WIT & WISDOM of the PRESIDENTS

CONTRIBUTING WRITER
ERIC ETHIER

ILLUSTRATORS
DAN KROVATIN
C. B. MORDAN
JOHN ZIELINSKI

PUBLICATIONS INTERNATIONAL, LTD.

Contributing Writer

Eric Ethier is the associate editor of *American History* magazine and is a freelance writer and researcher who specializes in the history of the Old West, the Civil War, and World War II. His work has appeared in periodicals such as *Civil War Times Illustrated, American History, Civil War News,* and *Rhode Island History.*

Illustrations: Dan Krovatin, C. B. Mordan, John Zielinski

Acknowledgments

Publications International, Ltd., has made every effort to locate the owners of all copyrighted material to obtain permission to use the selections that appear in this book. Any errors or omissions are unintentional; corrections, if necessary, will be made in future editions.

Page 11: Charles S. Olcott, *The Life of William McKinley, Vol. 1.* Copyright © 1916 by Houghton Mifflin Company.

Pages 11, 17, 45, 46, 48, 57, 121, 134, 139: From *The Complete Book of the U.S. Presidents.* Copyright © 1996 by William A. DeGregorio; 1996 update by Connie Jo Dickerson. Published by arrangement with Barricade Books, Inc., NY.

Pages 12, 30, 47, 65, 66, 121, 132: Excerpts from *Kennedy* by Theodore C. Sorensen. Copyright © 1965. Copyright renewed 1993 by Theodore C. Sorensen. Reprinted by permission of HarperCollins Publishers, Inc.

Pages 12, 29, 30, 39, 143, 151: Taken from Herbert Hoover Papers, Public Statements and Addresses, Herbert Hoover Presidential Library.

Pages 15, 25, 28, 37, 57, 62, 102: Excerpts from *A Thousand Days.* Copyright © 1965 by Arthur M. Schlesinger, Jr. Reprinted by permission of Houghton Mifflin Co. All rights reserved.

Pages 16, 51: Excerpts from *Gentleman Boss: The Life of Chester Alan Arthur* by Thomas C. Reeves. Copyright © 1975. Reprinted by permission of Alfred A. Knopf, Inc.

Pages 17, 62, 89: Excerpts from *Roosevelt To Reagan: A Reporter's Encounters with Nine Presidents* by Hedley Donovan. Copyright © 1985 by Hedley Donovan. Epilogue copyright © 1987 by Hedley Donovan. Reprinted by permission of HarperCollins Publishers, Inc.

Pages 17, 21, 29, 35, 99, 104, 112, 114, 119, 121, 123, 125, 127, 128, 151: Excerpts from *The Presidential Families,* by E. H. Gwynne-Thomas. Copyright © 1989. Published by Hippocrene Books, Inc. Used by permission.

Pages 19, 28, 31, 52, 93, 105, 109: Excerpts from *The Wit and Wisdom of Jimmy Carter* by Bill Alder. Copyright © 1977. Reprinted by permission of The Citadel Press.

Pages 22, 23, 24, 49, 70, 80, 96, 99, 100: From *The Presidential Character: Predicting Performance in the White House* by James David Barber. Copyright © 1972 by James David Barber. Prentice Hall Publishers. Used with permission of the author.

Pages 23, 24, 54, 113: Excerpts from *Looking Forward* by George Bush. Copyright © 1987. Published by Bantam Doubleday Dell Publishing Group, Inc.

Page 24: Excerpt from *The Rise of Warren Gamaliel Harding* by Randolph C. Downes. Copyright © 1970. Reprinted by permission of The Ohio State University Press.

Pages 29, 93, 118, 121: Taken from *The Come Back Kid* by Charles F. Allen and Jonathan Portis. Copyright © 1992. Reprinted by permission of Carol Publishing Group.

Pages 29, 56, 96, 154: Excerpts from *American Sphinx: The Character of Thomas Jefferson* by Joseph J. Ellis. Copyright © 1996. Reprinted by permission of Alfred A. Knopf, Inc.

Pages 30, 81, 117: From *The Truman Wit*, edited by Alex J. Goldman. Copyright © 1966. Reprinted by permission of The Citadel Press.

Page 40: Taken from *The Loneliest Campaign: The Truman Victory of 1948* by Irwin Ross. Copyright © 1968 by Irwin Ross. Reprinted by permission of Russell & Volkening as agents for the author.

Pages 47, 51, 90, 92, 93, 96: From *Speaker's Treasury of Political Stories, Anecdotes and Humor* by Gerald Tomlinson. Copyright © 1990. Reprinted with permission of Prentice Hall.

Pages 48, 62, 118: Excerpts from *Exit With Honor: The Life and Presidency of Ronald Reagan* by William E. Pemberton. Copyright © 1997. Reprinted with permission from M. E. Sharpe, Inc.

Pages 51, 146: Taken from *Letters of Thomas Jefferson* by Frank Irwin. Copyright © 1975. Used by permission of Sant Bani Press.

Page 73: From *On Reagan: The Man and His Presidency* by Ronnie Dugger. Copyright © 1983. Reproduced with permission from The McGraw-Hill Companies.

Pages 74, 83, 85, 106, 149: From *Theodore Roosevelt The Citizen* by Jacob A. Riis. Reprinted courtesy of AMS Press, Inc., reprinted 1969.

Page 82: From *The Kennedy Wit* by Bill Adler. Copyright © 1964. Reprinted by permission of The Citadel Press.

Pages 127, 135, 141: From *Presidents At Play*, copyright © 1995 by George Sullivan. Reprinted with permission from Walker and Company, 435 Hudson St., New York, NY 10014, 1-800-289-2553. All rights reserved.

Contents

The State of
the Union

ABRAHAM LINCOLN, who had once given up on
marriage because he could "never be satisfied with
anyone who would be blockhead enough to have
me," endeared himself to Americans with his self-
deprecating humor and folksy stories.

John F. Kennedy's witty one-liners were as memorable as his inspiring inaugural address. Tired of
defending his Catholic heritage during the 1960
campaign, Kennedy snapped, "Now I understand
why Henry VIII set up his own church."

Wit & Wisdom of the Presidents is a lighthearted
collection of quotes, anecdotes, facts, and trivia about
America's chief executives. Through public speeches,
off-the-cuff remarks, and private correspondence,
American presidents revealed their candid feelings
on politics, family, and life in general. This book
takes a look at their words, showing that presidents
are people too.

Life in the White House isn't easy. Chester
Arthur once moaned, "You have no idea how

depressing and fatiguing it is to live in the same house where you work." Harry S Truman constantly referred to the White House as the "Great White Jail," and many of his predecessors had been only too happy to leave it. Presidents have historically handled their problems like most people, however, with determination and a sense of humor.

"I don't recall," said Calvin Coolidge during the 1924 campaign, "any candidate for president that ever injured himself very much by not talking." "Silent Cal's" tight-lipped style apparently worked well for him, as he won the election handily. Today Coolidge is a member of that odd group of presidents—Buchanan, Pierce, Tyler, and Fillmore—who are remembered more for their almost comical obscurity than for anything they did or said. Yet it was Coolidge whom comedian Will Rogers found to have mastered the art of dry wit beyond any other politician he ever met. Of course, Coolidge was also scornfully referred to by Harry S Truman as the president "who got more rest than any previous president."

Soon after starting work on his autobiography, Thomas Jefferson admitted, "I am already tired of talking about myself." Fortunately, he and his presidential cohorts have said more than enough to keep Americans thinking and laughing today.

Electoral Collage

"**T**HESE REPUBLICAN LEADERS have
not been content with attacks on me, or
my wife, or on my sons. No, not content with
that, they now included my little dog, Fala.
Well, of course, I don't resent attacks,
and my family doesn't resent attacks,
but Fala *does* resent them.

—FRANKLIN ROOSEVELT, 1944, IN RESPONSE TO
CHARGES THAT HE HAD SENT A NAVY DESTROYER
TO PICK UP HIS DOG IN THE ALEUTIAN ISLANDS

Yes, Chicken?

Dᴜʀɪɴɢ ᴀ 1976 campaign stop in San Diego, President Gerald Ford was the target of a practical joke when a *New York Times* correspondent donned a costume of the San Diego Padres' mascot, the San Diego Chicken, and attended a news conference hosted by Ford. As the president fielded the reporters' questions, the head of the oversized bird suddenly appeared behind the group. Without cracking a smile, Ford pointed to the chicken and said, "Yes, you, that chicken in the back, do you have a question?"

"I ᴀᴍ ɴᴏᴛ of Caesar's mind. The second place in Rome is high enough for me."

—*Jᴏʜɴ Aᴅᴀᴍs, ʀᴇsᴘᴏɴᴅɪɴɢ ᴛᴏ ᴀᴄᴄᴜsᴀᴛɪᴏɴs ᴛʜᴀᴛ ʜᴇ ᴡᴀs ɢʀᴏᴏᴍɪɴɢ ʜɪᴍsᴇʟғ ᴛᴏ sᴜᴄᴄᴇᴇᴅ ᴛʜᴇɴ-Pʀᴇsɪᴅᴇɴᴛ Gᴇᴏʀɢᴇ Wᴀsʜɪɴɢᴛᴏɴ*

"I ᴋɴᴇᴡ that this job would be too much for me."

—*Wᴀʀʀᴇɴ G. Hᴀʀᴅɪɴɢ*

"**A**T FIRST I INTENDED to become a student of the Senate rules and I did learn much about them, but I soon found that the Senate had but one fixed rule, subject to exceptions of course, which was to the effect that the Senate would do anything it wanted to do whenever it wanted to do it."

—*CALVIN COOLIDGE, 1929, RECALLING HIS DAYS AS VICE PRESIDENT AND PRESIDENT OF THE SENATE*

"**A**H, MY FRIEND, my fidelity to my constituents is not measured by the support they give me!"

—*WILLIAM MCKINLEY, 1883, IN RESPONSE TO A COMMENT THAT HIS FELLOW OHIOANS HAD NOT FULLY SUPPORTED HIM IN THE PREVIOUS CONGRESSIONAL ELECTION, WHICH MCKINLEY HAD WON BY JUST EIGHT VOTES*

"**I** SIT HERE all day trying to persuade people to do the things they ought to have sense enough to do without my persuading them. . . . That's all the powers of the president amount to."

—*HARRY S TRUMAN*

"**S**O I COME here today full of admiration for Senator Johnson, full of affection for him, strongly in support of him—for Majority Leader."

—*JOHN F. KENNEDY, 1960, ON SENATE MAJORITY LEADER LYNDON JOHNSON, WHO WAS ALSO SEEKING THE DEMOCRATIC NOMINATION FOR PRESIDENT*

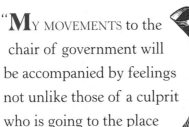

"**M**Y MOVEMENTS to the chair of government will be accompanied by feelings not unlike those of a culprit who is going to the place of his execution."

—*GEORGE WASHINGTON, 1789, ON ASSUMING THE PRESIDENCY*

"**O**UR STANDARDS of material progress include the notion and the hope that we shall lessen the daily hours of labor on the farm, at the bench, and in the office—except for public servants."

—*HERBERT HOOVER, 1927*

"**N**O PRESIDENT who performs his duties faithfully and conscientiously can have any leisure."

—*JAMES K. POLK, 1847*

"**M**Y GOD, what is there in this place that a man should ever want to get into it?"

—*JAMES A. GARFIELD, 1881,*
REFERRING TO THE WHITE HOUSE

"**M**Y DEAR SIR, if you are as happy on entering the White House as I am on leaving, you are a very happy man indeed."

—*JAMES BUCHANAN, 1861, TO HIS SUCCESSOR,*
ABRAHAM LINCOLN

"**N**EVER DID a prisoner, released from his chains, feel such relief as I shall on shaking off the shackles of power."

—*THOMAS JEFFERSON, CONTEMPLATING*
THE END OF HIS PRESIDENCY

An Act of Grace

ABRAHAM LINCOLN was the first bearded president, a distinction that was inspired by an 11-year-old girl named Grace Bedell. In October 1860, Grace wrote to the future president and encouraged him to grow "whiskers," an act she thought might encourage her brothers to vote for him. Lincoln responded soon after. "As to the whiskers," he wrote, "having never worn any, do you not think people would call it a piece of silly affectation if I were to begin it now?"

Lincoln did grow a beard, however, and on the way to his inauguration in 1861 he had his train stop in Grace's hometown of Westfield, New York, where he met his young friend and told the assembled crowd, "She wrote me that she thought I'd look better if I wore whiskers."

"EVERY MAN has a few mental hair shirts... presidents differ only by their larger wardrobe."
—*HERBERT HOOVER, 1930*

"**I** CAN WITH TRUTH say mine is a situation of
dignified slavery."

—*ANDREW JACKSON, 1829*

"**R**EAD my lips: No new taxes."

—*GEORGE BUSH, 1988. WHEN HE EVENTUALLY DID
RAISE TAXES, HE HAD TO EAT HIS WORDS.*

"**L**ET'S NOT talk so much about vice.
I'm against vice, in all forms."

—*JOHN F. KENNEDY, 1958, ON A COMMENT THAT THE VICE
PRESIDENTIAL NOMINATION WAS HIS FOR THE TAKING*

"**I** HOPE I SHALL always possess firmness
and virtue enough to maintain (what I consider
the most enviable of all titles) the character
of an 'honest man.'"

—*GEORGE WASHINGTON, FROM HIS
1796 FAREWELL ADDRESS*

"**T**HE SECOND OFFICE of the land is honorable and easy, the first is but a splendid misery."

—*THOMAS JEFFERSON, 1797*

"**Y**OU HAVE no idea how depressing and fatiguing it is to live in the same house where you work."

—*CHESTER ARTHUR, 1884. PRESIDENT ARTHUR'S WORK ETHIC WAS SAID TO BE LESS THAN DILIGENT.*

"**F**OR THE HIGH HONOR and responsibilities of such an office . . . I have not the slightest aspiration."

—*ZACHARY TAYLOR, 1847, ON THE PRESIDENCY. HE WAS ELECTED THE FOLLOWING YEAR.*

"**M**Y COUNTRY has in its wisdom contrived for me the most insignificant office that ever the invention of man contrived or his imagination conceived."

—*JOHN ADAMS, 1793, ON THE VICE PRESIDENCY*

"I COULDN'T wait to start the day."
—*GERALD FORD, ON THE PRESIDENCY*

"DON'T SIT UP nights thinking about making me President, for that will never come and I have no ambition in that direction. Any party which would nominate me would make a great mistake."
—*WILLIAM HOWARD TAFT, 1903*

"WELL BOYS, your troubles are over now, mine have just begun."
—*PRESIDENT-ELECT ABRAHAM LINCOLN, TO REPORTERS*

"YOU WON'T have Nixon to kick around anymore, because, gentlemen, this is my last press conference."
—*RICHARD NIXON, FOLLOWING HIS 1962 DEFEAT IN THE CALIFORNIA GOVERNOR'S RACE*

"**I** AM NOT going to exploit, for political purposes, my opponent's youth and inexperience."

—*RONALD REAGAN, 1984. REAGAN'S 56-YEAR-OLD CAMPAIGN OPPONENT, WALTER MONDALE, HAD RAISED THE PRESIDENT'S AGE AS A CAMPAIGN ISSUE. REAGAN WAS 73 AT THE TIME.*

"**I**T WILL GIVE me philosophical evenings in the winter, and rural days in summer."

—*THOMAS JEFFERSON, 1796, ON THE VICE PRESIDENCY*

"**S**ERIOUSLY, I do not think I am fit for the Presidency."

—*ABRAHAM LINCOLN, 1859*

"**I**F YOU THINK too much about being reelected, it is very difficult to be worth reelecting."

—*WOODROW WILSON, 1913*

"I AM NO big shot. I am not anybody's boss. I want
to be everybody's servant."

—*JIMMY CARTER, 1976*

"IT SEEMS to be the profession of a president simply
to hear other people talk."

—*WILLIAM HOWARD TAFT, 1910*

"THIS JOB is nothing but a twenty-ring circus—
with a whole lot of bad actors."

—*HERBERT HOOVER*

Speech, Speech

WILLIAM MCKINLEY was meticulous in his preparations for speeches, often carrying a thick pile of notes with him to the podium. He could usually be counted on to say something significant. On one occasion early in his career, however, he was caught speechless.

McKinley was asked to speak from the same platform as Charles F. Manderson, who later became a senator from Nebraska. Manderson's speaking habits were precisely the opposite of young McKinley's; he seldom prepared for an address, speaking instead from memory or as the occasion inspired him. On this day, Manderson remarked to his colleague that he was unacquainted with the issues at hand and asked McKinley to tell him the gist of his own speech. McKinley obliged by reading his address to Manderson and showing him various documents and statistics he had brought along for the occasion.

Impressed, Manderson said, "Major, you've got this in pretty good shape, and I'm only going to speak offhand. Don't you think you'd better let me be the 'curtain-raiser' and lead off?" McKinley agreed.

Manderson took the stage and promptly launched into a speech the surprised McKinley immediately recognized as his own. He listened as the audience applauded each of his points, aware that all he would be left with was his statistics. Finally, in a perfect conclusion to the odd affair, Manderson finished "his" address by turning to McKinley and saying to the crowd, "And now, gentlemen, in proof of all I have told you, we have taken pains to collect some interesting figures and other documentary evidence, and if my distinguished colleague will kindly hand me the papers which he has in his pocket, I will read them to you."

McKinley learned his lesson and from then on kept his speeches to himself.

"I AM VICE PRESIDENT. In this I am nothing.
But I may be everything."
—JOHN ADAMS

"IT IS a very nice prison, but a prison nevertheless."
—HARRY S TRUMAN, ON THE WHITE HOUSE

"SOME DAY, when I leave this Great White Jail,
I want to sit with you and discuss history from
1920 to 1953. We can have a great time."

—*HARRY S TRUMAN, 1952, FROM AN UNMAILED LETTER TO
FORMER U.S. AMBASSADOR TO GREECE HENRY F. GRADY*

"I HAVE A NICE HOME. The office is close by
and the pay is good."

—*JOHN F. KENNEDY, ON THE WHITE HOUSE*

"**H**UBERT is too intense for the present mood of the people. He gets people too excited, too worked up.... What they want today is a more boring, monotonous personality, like me."

—*JOHN F. KENNEDY, 1960, ON HIS OPPONENT FOR THE DEMOCRATIC PRESIDENTIAL NOMINATION, HUBERT HUMPHREY*

"**J**OHN ADAMS CLAIMED he was miserable in the job. Then he became President and did his best to make *his* Vice President, Thomas Jefferson, miserable. A century later Teddy Roosevelt liked to repeat Mark Twain's joke about the two brothers: One went to sea and the other became Vice President. Neither was ever heard from again."

—*GEORGE BUSH, FROM HIS AUTOBIOGRAPHY, LOOKING FORWARD*

"**O**NE OF THE MOST appalling trials which confront a president is the perpetual clamor for public utterances."

—*CALVIN COOLIDGE*

"No MAN who ever held the office of president would congratulate a friend on obtaining it."

—*JOHN ADAMS, 1824, TO HIS SON JOHN QUINCY ADAMS, WHO HAD JUST BEEN ELECTED PRESIDENT*

"UNDECIDED. Put her down as a firm undecided."

—*GEORGE BUSH, 1980, ON A HECKLER WHO HAD ANGRILY TOLD HIM, "I WOULDN'T VOTE FOR YOU IF CASTRO WAS RUNNING!"*

"THE ONLY THING I really worry about is that I am sometimes very much afraid I am going to be nominated and elected. That's an awful thing to contemplate."

—*WARREN G. HARDING, 1919*

"THE ONLY THING that really surprised us when we got into office was that things were just as bad as we had been saying they were."

—*JOHN F. KENNEDY, 1961*

"**P**OLITICS MAKES me sick."
—*WILLIAM HOWARD TAFT*

"**I** SPOKE almost every day till the election, but it now appears that we are defeated by the combined power of rebellion, Catholicism and whiskey, a trinity very hard to conquer."
—*JAMES A. GARFIELD, 1876*

"**T**HERE IS one thing about this job. It has no future to it. Every young man wants something to look forward to."
—*HARRY S TRUMAN*

"**W**ELL, JUST PUT me down as a lawyer; I want that known because I may need the business soon."
—*WILLIAM HOWARD TAFT, 1912, TO A TOWN CLERK AT A VOTING BOOTH WHO HAD ASKED HIS PROFESSION*

I Play a Politician on TV

As a student at Whittier College, Richard Nixon took drama classes and developed into a decent actor. His drama teacher, Professor Albert Upton, later recalled how he had feared that his pupil would be unable to summon the tears necessary for an emotional scene in the play *Bird in Hand.* On the night of the performance, however, Upton watched the crucial scene with glee as Nixon wept on cue. Years later, Nixon the politician said in an interview that he never cried except in public before an audience.

In 1952, after saving his vice presidential slot on the Republican ticket with Dwight D. Eisenhower by making his famed "Checkers" speech on television, Nixon leaned on Senator William Knowland and cried openly. Upton, watching the scene at home on his television, exulted, "That's my boy! That's my actor!"

"IT IS BETTER to be defeated battling for an honest principle than to win by a cowardly subterfuge."

—GROVER CLEVELAND, AFTER LOSING THE 1888 ELECTION TO BENJAMIN HARRISON. CLEVELAND WAS ELECTED AGAIN FOUR YEARS LATER.

"I SEE that one of my adversaries has lost his head."

—WILLIAM HOWARD TAFT, AFTER SOMEONE HAD THROWN A CABBAGE AT HIM DURING A CAMPAIGN STOP

"I AM BIDDING goodbye to private life and to a long series of happy years which I fear terminate in 1880."

—JAMES A. GARFIELD, ON WINNING THE PRESIDENCY

"MY OWN SITUATION [the vice presidency] is almost the only one in the world in which firmness and patience are useless."

—JOHN ADAMS

Nothing to Worry About

THE GOOD-HUMORED Gerald Ford made himself
his own target in some of the many witty stories and
jokes he told. One of his favorite anecdotes centered
on a speech he made in Omaha, Nebraska. At a
reception he attended following his speech, a friendly
old lady approached him and, taking Ford's hand,
said "I hear you spoke here tonight."

"Oh, it was nothing," Ford replied.

"Yes," replied the old lady, as she nodded in
agreement, "that's what I heard."

"IF ALL THE THINGS the Republicans are saying
about me are true, I wouldn't vote for myself either."
—JIMMY CARTER, 1976

"OK, IF I WIN this election, I will have won it
myself, but, if I lose, you fellows will have lost it.
—JOHN F. KENNEDY, 1960, TO MEMBERS OF HIS STAFF

"I'M SURE they're here and I'm not half so alarmed at meeting up with any of them as I am at having to meet the live nuts I have to see every day."
—*HARRY S TRUMAN, ON WHITE HOUSE "GHOSTS"*

"GOVERNMENT'S RESPONSIBILITY is to create more opportunity. The people's responsibility is to make the most of it."
—*BILL CLINTON*

"YOU WILL EXPECT me to discuss the late election. Well, as nearly as I can learn, we did not have enough votes on our side."
—*HERBERT HOOVER, FOLLOWING HIS 1932 ELECTION LOSS TO FRANKLIN ROOSEVELT*

"I AM every day convinced that neither my talents, tone of mind, nor time of life fit me for public life."
—*THOMAS JEFFERSON, 1794*

"**I** DON'T WANT to be vice president. I bet I can go down on the street and stop the first ten men I see, and that they can't tell me the names of two of the last ten vice presidents of the United States."
—*HARRY S TRUMAN, 1944*

"**I**'M ONE of those who can truthfully say,
'I got my job through *The New York Times*.'"
—*JOHN F. KENNEDY, ON THE INFLUENTIAL NEWSPAPER
WHOSE SUPPORT HE HAD RECEIVED DURING
THE 1960 CAMPAIGN*

"**I**NCIDENTALLY, you could discover from these proceedings why presidents seldom worry about anything. They have so many troubles in the closet or stowed away in the ice box that when one of them gets tiresome they can always send for another, and by great variety maintain interest and a high cheerfulness of spirit."
—*HERBERT HOOVER, 1929*

Nun-Sense

DURING ONE of Bill Clinton's early campaigns, an aide who was soliciting votes for the future president telephoned a nun who had once taught Clinton in elementary school. The nun gave Clinton the strongest of endorsements, saying, "If he wants to be president, then he's going to be president." The aide asked her for support in the upcoming election, and the nun answered, "My goodness, you've had my support since he was in the second grade!"

"**I** DON'T CLAIM to be the man best qualified to be President of the United States. There are, right here in this room, people better qualified to be president than I am. And I want to thank you for not running this year: I've already got competition enough."

—*JIMMY CARTER, 1976*

Sic Semper Tyrannis

As a GENIAL and well-mannered young boy, John Tyler was gentle in nature and managed to get along well with everyone. Beneath his somewhat soft exterior, however, lay strength in character. Around the age of ten, Tyler was attending a small school where the teacher was an extremely harsh man named McMurdo. So strict in his discipline was McMurdo that, as Tyler later recalled, "it was a wonder that he did not whip all the sense out of his scholars." One day, after having had enough of their teacher's tyrannical methods, the students rose in revolt.

With Tyler taking charge, the boys overpowered McMurdo, tied his hands and feet together, and left him locked in the schoolroom. The humiliated teacher remained in his bound position until late in the day, when a passerby released him. Incensed, McMurdo went straight to Tyler's house and informed his father of the situation. A federal judge, Mr. Tyler nevertheless was surprised and delighted in the bold stand his son had taken and sent the teacher away with the Virginia state motto *Sic Semper Tyrannis* ("Thus be it always to tyrants") ringing in his ears.

Years later, when Tyler assumed the presidency following the sudden death of William Henry Harrison, he found himself besieged by politicians who had the mistaken impression that he was easily manipulated. Henry Clay and Daniel Webster, two powerful Washington figures with designs on the presidency, were among his challengers. In one of Tyler's first cabinet meetings, Secretary of State Webster hinted that the cabinet members were to have as much influence in decision-making as the president. Tyler paused for only a moment before setting things straight. He respected their abilities and opinions, he stated, but he was responsible for the administration and would not be dictated to. "I shall be glad to have you with me," he said firmly, and added "when you think otherwise, your resignations will be accepted." The politicians got the message.

"SPEAKING OF the religious issue, I asked the Chief Justice tonight whether he thought our new educational bill was constitutional. He said, 'It's clearly constitutional. It hasn't got a prayer.'"
—*JOHN F. KENNEDY, 1963*

Late for Dinner

JOHN F. KENNEDY hated to lose. Once, at a Boston Red Sox game in 1946, he asked an assistant, Dave Powers, what the odds were against slugger Ted Williams hitting a home run in his next at-bat. Fifteen to one, Powers said. Kennedy then bet Powers that Williams would not homer on his next at-bat. On Williams's next swing, he belted the ball out of the park, sending Powers and the rest of the crowd to their feet cheering. Kennedy hung his head dejectedly and said nothing for the next two innings.

Kennedy applied this competitive spirit to his political campaigns with unmatched vigor. His staff members were often amazed by the candidate's drive. During the late 1940s, when travel was far less convenient than it is today, the congressman and his aides spent a lot of time on the road, staying in low-budget hotels with poor lighting and often unsanitary bathrooms. After a speaking engagement in Danvers, Massachusetts, Kennedy sent an aide to a drugstore for a razor and shaving cream. The future president quickly shaved in the bathroom of a local bowling alley, squinting into a shoddy, old mirror, before rushing off to make another speech. An assistant later remembered Kennedy as "the only guy I ever knew who could shave while wearing his topcoat."

After several years in politics, Kennedy got used to traveling and came to regard even long trips as mere jaunts. On one occasion, Kennedy called and asked Powers to join him on a "short trip." Powers told his wife as he left his Massachusetts home that he would be home for dinner. When he called home later, Mrs. Powers told him that dinner was waiting and asked him where he was. Powers replied that he would have to miss the meal, as he and Kennedy were at a Jefferson Day Dinner in Des Moines, Iowa!

"I DON'T KNOW whether I am glad or not."
—*JAMES A. GARFIELD, 1880, ON HIS NOMINATION FOR THE PRESIDENCY*

"I TREAD IN the footsteps of illustrious men, whose superiors it is our happiness to believe are not found on the executive calendar of any country."
—*MARTIN VAN BUREN, FROM HIS 1837 INAUGURAL ADDRESS*

And the Winner is . . .

THE ONLY PERSON who gave Harry Truman a chance to win the 1948 presidential election was the incumbent himself. All the polls showed Republican Thomas Dewey well ahead in the race; one poll had even shut down for the campaign since any further canvassing seemed a waste of time. Nevertheless, Truman crisscrossed the country by train, making countless whistle-stops and gradually rallying the populace to his side. When Truman's train stopped in Indiana three weeks before the election, presidential aide Clark Clifford entered the train station in search of the latest issue of *Newsweek*. The magazine contained the opinions of prominent political journalists who had been asked to predict who would win the election. All 50 writers picked Dewey to win.

Hoping to keep the bad news to himself, Clifford climbed back aboard the train only to immediately encounter the president, who was casually scanning the morning papers. As Truman was well aware of the poll, Clifford reluctantly handed over the magazine. After briefly scanning the article, Truman said to his aide, "I know every one of these 50 fellows. There isn't one of them has enough sense to pound sand in a rat hole."

Truman won the election.

"My EXPERIENCE in government is that when things are noncontroversial, beautifully coordinated, and all the rest, it must be that not much is going on."

—*JOHN F. KENNEDY*

"I HAVE TO TELL you with complete candor that being elected president is not the most important thing in my life. There are many...things that I would not do to be president."

—*JIMMY CARTER, 1974*

"I PINCH MYSELF every little while to make myself realize that it is all true."

—*WILLIAM HOWARD TAFT, AFTER BEING ELECTED PRESIDENT*

Senate Scenes

AFTER BECOMING Andrew Jackson's vice president in 1832, Martin Van Buren found himself at odds with old political foes who resented his connection to the president. As the vice president presided over the Senate, Henry Clay, an ardent opponent of President Jackson's banking policies, took the Senate floor and directed a transparent, politically motivated speech at Van Buren.

As Clay stood before the assemblage, he put on a wonderful performance. Speaking with passion, he spoke at length of how the poor were being ruined by Jackson's unfair fiscal policies. Clay expected his message to be taken directly to the president, but he was surprised when Van Buren, exhibiting firmness, composure, and even a dry sense of humor, resisted.

Van Buren watched quietly, "looking respectfully and even innocently at the speaker as if treasuring up every word." Finally, Clay finished speaking and strode back to his chair, practically in tears from his theatrical effort. The Senate prepared for a response from the vice president; it seemed impossible for him to resist such an impassioned argument.

Van Buren appeared to be on the hot seat. Ever mindful of his own political fortunes, Van Buren had kept a fair distance from Jackson's banking policies. His colleagues were well aware of his reluctance to commit himself to a position, but the vice president was now cornered, and the time had apparently come for him to show his hand. Van Buren stood up and proceeded down to the floor as expected. Instead of approaching the dais to begin his response, however, he walked up the aisle and asked Clay for a pinch of snuff. Upon receiving the snuff, he cordially thanked the surprised Clay, then continued on up the aisle and right out of the Senate chamber.

"WE HAD A GOOD FIGHT, and when our opponents recover from the glow of victory and undertake to perform the sad rites of burying their dead promises, that will be another story. And the Republicans will, no doubt, take care of that."

—*HERBERT HOOVER, 1932*

Presidential Seals of Approval

"**I** WOULDN'T throw *fresh* eggs at Taft."

—HARRY S TRUMAN, 1948, RESPONDING TO A
SUPPORTER'S JOKING QUESTION OF WHETHER HE
WOULD HURL EGGS AT HIS OPPONENT, ROBERT TAFT.
TRUMAN HAD BEEN PRESENTED WITH A GIFT BASKET
OF EGGS DURING A CAMPAIGN WHISTLE-STOP.

A "Religious" Man

DURING AND AFTER the Civil War, Abraham Lincoln commuted the death sentences of many Union Army deserters and received countless appeals for leniency from the relatives of Confederate prisoners. The kindly president's reputation for mercy and fairness was well known. He managed, however, to make a stern point with people in other ways.

In 1864, the wives of two Confederate soldiers from Tennessee asked him to have their husbands released from a federal prison. One of the women, in hopes of swaying Lincoln's feelings, stressed the fact that her husband was a religious man. Lincoln released the men, but asked the wife of the "religious" man to tell her husband, "I am not much of a judge of religion; but . . . in my opinion, the religion that sets men to rebel and fight against their government, because, as they think, that government does not sufficiently help some men to eat their bread in the sweat of other men's faces, is not the sort of religion upon which people can get to heaven."

"**G**ARFIELD HAS SHOWN me that he is not possessed
of the backbone of an angle-worm."
—*ULYSSES S. GRANT, 1881*

"**M**AY GOD SAVE the country; for it is
evident the people will not."
—*MILLARD FILLMORE, FOLLOWING THE
1844 ELECTION OF JAMES K. POLK*

"**H**OW MANY OF YOU have relatives in America
whom you'd admit to?"
—*JOHN F. KENNEDY, FROM A 1963 SPEECH IN IRELAND*

"**I**N A BODY where there are more than one
hundred talking lawyers, you can make no
calculation upon the termination upon any debate
and frequently, the more trifling the subject, the
more animated and protracted the discussion."
—*FRANKLIN PIERCE, ON CONGRESS*

"TAFT MEANT WELL, but he meant well feebly."
—*THEODORE ROOSEVELT, ON WILLIAM HOWARD TAFT*

"BEST OF LUCK and may the honest Democrats and Liberal Republicans save you from disaster."
—*HARRY S TRUMAN, FROM AN UNMAILED, 1956 MESSAGE TO HIS SUCCESSOR, DWIGHT D. EISENHOWER*

"HE LIVES AND WILL LIVE in memory and gratitude of the wise and good, as a luminary of science, as a votary of liberty, as a model of patriotism, and as a benefactor of human kind."
—*JAMES MADISON, 1826, IN MEMORY OF THOMAS JEFFERSON*

"**M**ERCHANTS love nobody."
—*THOMAS JEFFERSON, 1785*

"**I**F YOU WANT to send a man to the moon, send a Peace Corps member up there. It's an underdeveloped country."
—*DWIGHT D. EISENHOWER*

"**P**IERCE WAS THE BEST looking President the White House ever had—but as President he ranks with Buchanan and Calvin Coolidge."
—*HARRY S TRUMAN, 1952*

"**L**ET THEM COMPLAIN. It's too easy for them to get up here the way it is."
—*WILLIAM McKINLEY, REPLYING TO COMPLAINTS OF CONGRESSMEN THAT THE WHITE HOUSE ELEVATOR WAS BROKEN*

The Man Who Came to Dinner

RENOWNED *New York Times* correspondent Arthur Krock hosted a dinner party for diplomats, politicians, and their wives one evening in the 1950s. One of the guests—a well-known, older gentleman—revealed a remarkable breadth of knowledge, a keen sense of humor, and considerable charm over the course of the evening. The man's character surprised many of his fellow diners, whose prior impression of him had been formed largely through newspaper stories and unfair criticism. When the aging gentleman departed at the end of the night, a senator's wife exclaimed with astonishment, "That just can't be Herbert Hoover."

It was.

"I DON'T KNOW what to do or where to turn in this taxation matter. Somewhere there must be a book that tells all about it, where I could go to straighten it out in my mind. But I don't know where the book is, and maybe I couldn't read it if I found it!"

—WARREN G. HARDING, 1923

"I AM READING more and enjoying it less."
—JOHN F. KENNEDY, ON THE PRESS

"[JEFFERSON WAS] PERHAPS the most incapable
executive that ever filled the presidential chair. . . . It
would be difficult to imagine a man less fit to guide a
state with honor and safety through the stormy times
that marked the opening of the present century."
—THEODORE ROOSEVELT, 1882, ON THOMAS JEFFERSON

"LEGISLATORS BLINDLY FOLLOW leaders.
Sometimes the bellwether is trustworthy;
sometimes he is an old goat."
—WOODROW WILSON, 1910

"RONALD REAGAN doesn't dye his hair—
he's just prematurely orange."
—GERALD FORD

"[WILLIAM] McKINLEY has no more
backbone than a chocolate eclair."
—*THEODORE ROOSEVELT, 1897*

"YOU [BUSINESSMEN] WASTE a lot of money hiring
lawyers to tell you how to avoid the law. Has it never
occurred to you that you could save money by hiring
lawyers to tell you how you can conform to the law?"
—*WOODROW WILSON, 1912, FROM A SPEECH GIVEN
TO THE NEWARK BOARD OF TRADE*

"THAT MAN HAS OFFERED me unsolicited advice for
the past six years, all of it bad."
—*CALVIN COOLIDGE, ON HERBERT HOOVER*

"IT'S TRUE HARD WORK never killed anybody, but
I figure, why take a chance?"
—*RONALD REAGAN*

"I DON'T BELIEVE the American people want a gelding in the White House."

—GROVER CLEVELAND, RESPONDING TO CHARGES THAT HE HAD FATHERED AN ILLEGITIMATE CHILD

"YOU CAN'T MAKE a Teddy Roosevelt out of me."

—HERBERT HOOVER

"HOW WE NEED the old building across the street, known as the White House. If Theodore Roosevelt and old man Coolidge had done as they should, we wouldn't be out doors now!"

—HARRY S TRUMAN, FROM A 1949 DIARY ENTRY. WITH THE WHITE HOUSE BEING RENOVATED, THE PRESIDENT HAD BEEN TEMPORARILY RELOCATED TO THE NEARBY BLAIR-LEE HOUSE.

President of Outer Space

JOHN F. KENNEDY employed his wit wisely throughout his career, directing good-natured but clever barbs at political foes to great effect. Lyndon Baines Johnson, the Texas native who opposed Kennedy in the 1960 race for the Democratic presidential nomination and later became his vice president, occasionally was the object of Kennedy's jokes. Johnson wielded a great deal of power during his days as Senate majority leader, and his ego sometimes reflected that.

At a 1958 Gridiron Club dinner in Washington, D.C., Kennedy poked fun at his Senate colleagues, telling the audience of a dream he had had in which God had entered his bedroom, anointed his head, and appointed him President of the United States. Kennedy continued, "Stuart Symington said, 'That's strange, Jack, because I too had a similar dream last night in which the Lord anointed me and declared me, Stuart Symington, President of the United States and Outer Space.' Lyndon Johnson said, 'That's very interesting, gentlemen, because I too had a similar dream last night and I don't remember anointing either of you.'"

"**C**ONSERVATISM IS THE POLICY of make no change
and consult your grandmother when in doubt."
—*WOODROW WILSON, 1918*

"**N**OTHING LIKE IT ever before in the Executive
Mansion—liquor, snobbery, and worse."
—*RUTHERFORD B. HAYES, ON THE GLAMOUR OF
THE CHESTER ARTHUR WHITE HOUSE*

"**I** MAY FURTHER SAY that I have not observed men's
honesty to increase with their riches."
—*THOMAS JEFFERSON, 1800*

"**A**nd the new president then pretty much
slept through the next six years, earning
himself the reputation of the man who got
more rest than any other president."
—*HARRY S TRUMAN, ON CALVIN COOLIDGE*

"LAST NIGHT when I was commenting on the FBI and the CIA the sound went off for twenty-seven minutes. I should have known better."
—*JIMMY CARTER, 1976*

"RESOLVE TO BE HONEST at all events: and if in your judgment you cannot be an honest lawyer, resolve to be honest without being a lawyer. Choose some other occupation."
—*ABRAHAM LINCOLN, 1850*

"**T**HE REPUBLIC . . . may suffer under the present imbecile chief, but the sober second thought of the people will restore it at our next presidential election."

—*ANDREW JACKSON, 1841, ON WILLIAM HENRY HARRISON*

"**W**E KNOW THAT our opponents will invoke the name of Abraham Lincoln on behalf of their candidate, despite the fact that his political career has often seemed to show charity towards none and malice towards all."

—*JOHN F. KENNEDY, 1960, ON HIS PRESIDENTIAL CAMPAIGN OPPONENT RICHARD NIXON*

"**I**F THESE SO CALLED "liberals" do what was done in 1948 we'll have that greatest of great synthetic liberals, the Hon. Richard Nixon for President. Do you want him? Of course you don't."

—*HARRY S TRUMAN, FROM AN UNMAILED, 1960 LETTER TO JOSEPH CLARK*

"OF COURSE, and the children have a sandpile.
You boys can play in it, if you like."

—*FRANKLIN DELANO ROOSEVELT, FROM A 1933 PRESS
CONFERENCE IN WHICH HE WAS ASKED IF REPORTERS
WOULD BE ALLOWED TO USE THE NEW WHITE HOUSE
SWIMMING POOL AND TENNIS COURTS*

"A FRIEND OF MINE says that every man who takes
office in Washington either grows or swells, and
when I give a man an office, I watch him carefully to
see whether he is swelling or growing. The mischief
of it is that when they swell they do not swell
enough to burst."

—*WOODROW WILSON, 1916*

"HE WAS A MAN, in short, who always seemed to
have his guard up. Jimmy Carter might have been
the European foreign minister who, on hearing that
Prince Metternich had just died, asked, 'I wonder
what he meant by that?'"

—*GEORGE BUSH, FROM HIS AUTOBIOGRAPHY,*
LOOKING FORWARD

The Right Hand of God

IN THE YEARS FOLLOWING his departure from the
White House, Harry Truman came to enjoy the role
of occasional tour guide at the Harry S Truman
Library in Independence, Missouri. He reveled in
making dry-humored remarks as he pointed out
various objects of interest to visitors. He often made
himself the butt of his own jokes: Pointing to a
portrait of himself in full Masonic garb, he would
identify it by saying, "And there's the Pope." This
usually drew a laugh from the crowd.

His favorite target, however, was Douglas
MacArthur, the insubordinate general Truman had
fired in 1951. When Truman led tourists past an
exhibit dedicated to famous generals and admirals, he
would sometimes point at and name them all except
for MacArthur. When his audience voiced curiosity
over the omission, the delighted ex-president would
casually acknowledge MacArthur's photograph with
a wave of his hand and sarcastically note, "And there's
the right hand of God."

The Washington Monument

DURING THE 1920s, when historical debunking was in vogue, the legacies of many prominent Americans came under attack. George Washington's reputation in particular was scrutinized. During a 1926 press conference, a reporter asked President Calvin Coolidge to comment on the personal habits of Washington, who had recently been disparaged. Coolidge coolly made known his thoughts about the first president by pointing out the window and saying, "The monument is still there."

"IT IS MARVELLOUS how political Plants grow in the shade."

—JOHN ADAMS

"**D**O YOU REALIZE the responsibility I carry? I'm the only person standing between Nixon and the White House."

—*JOHN F. KENNEDY, 1960*

"**I**KE DIDN'T KNOW ANYTHING, and all the time he was in office he didn't learn a thing."

—*HARRY S TRUMAN, 1961, ON DWIGHT D. EISENHOWER*

"**H**E HUNTS one half of the day, is drunk the other, and signs whatever he is bid."

—*THOMAS JEFFERSON, 1787, ON KING LOUIS XVI OF FRANCE*

"**F**IND OUT what he drinks and send a barrel of it to my other generals."

—*ABRAHAM LINCOLN, RESPONDING TO CHARGES THAT GENERAL (AND FUTURE PRESIDENT) ULYSSES S. GRANT HAD BEEN DRINKING. GRANT WAS THEN EMERGING AS THE UNION'S BEST GENERAL DURING THE CIVIL WAR.*

The Right Man for the Job

DESPITE THEIR MANY DIFFERENCES in philosophy, President Lincoln appointed Edwin Stanton Secretary of War. Stanton was immensely stubborn and generally wanted things done his way, and he often butted heads with his patient boss. The following exchange of memoranda between the two represents their often-contentious relationship during the Civil War:

Dear Mr. Stanton: Appoint this man chaplain in the army. A. Lincoln.

Dear Mr. Lincoln: He is not a preacher. E. M. Stanton.

Dear Mr. Stanton: He is now. . . . A. Lincoln.

Dear Mr. Lincoln: But there is no vacancy. E. M. Stanton.

Dear Mr. Stanton: Appoint him chaplain-at-large. A. Lincoln.

Dear Mr. Lincoln: There is no warrant for that. E. M. Stanton.

Dear Mr. Stanton: Appoint him anyhow. A. Lincoln.

Dear Mr. Lincoln: I will not. E. M. Stanton.

A visitor to Lincoln's office once told the president that his war secretary had referred to him as a "damned fool." Because Lincoln never lost sight of the ultimate goal, he overlooked such indiscretions. Stanton was the right man for the job—honest and a staunch Unionist—and Lincoln did not mind enduring a few barbs for the sake of the country. With his usual patience, he responded to this news by noting, "If Secretary Stanton called me a damned fool, then I probably am one, for the Secretary is usually right."

As the war progressed, the two men developed a strong admiration for each other and formed an effective partnership. When Lincoln died on April 15, 1865, it was a teary-eyed Secretary Stanton who offered the ultimate tribute to his one-time adversary: "Now he belongs to the ages."

I Do Solemnly Swear

FORMER JOHN F. KENNEDY AIDE and chief speech-writer Ted Sorenson recalled a brief conversation he had with the generally mild Richard Nixon. The day after Kennedy's famous 1961 inaugural address, Nixon approached Sorenson and admitted that he wished he had said some of the things his former Democratic foe had said on the previous day. Sorenson thanked him and asked him if he was referring to the "ask not what your country can do for you" part. "No, no, no," Nixon replied, "I mean the part about 'I do solemnly swear.'"

"I FELT THAT IF I met another monarch
I should bite him."

—*THEODORE ROOSEVELT, 1910, ON MEETING
A SERIES OF EUROPEAN SOVEREIGNS AT THE
FUNERAL OF ENGLAND'S KING EDWARD VII*

"I'M A FORD, not a Lincoln."

—*GERALD FORD, 1973*

"**I** DON'T THINK that the financial advisor of God Himself would be able to understand what the financial position of the Government of the United States is, by reading your statement."

—*HARRY S TRUMAN, FROM AN UNSENT, 1961 LETTER TO THE U.S. TREASURY DEPARTMENT. TRUMAN WAS ACCUSTOMED TO "PLAIN" SPEAKING.*

Relief in Belgium

IN 1919, Mr. and Mrs. Herbert Hoover accompanied President and Mrs. Woodrow Wilson and the king and queen of Belgium on a limousine ride through the Belgian countryside. At one point well into the ride, the limo driver pulled the car over, and its occupants scrambled out, with the men and women entering the woods separately. According to Hoover, the normally solemn and straightlaced Woodrow Wilson muttered to him, "Now I know the meaning of 'relief in Belgium.'"

Hoover, in turn, snapped, "I'm sorry it took you four years to find out."

"**N**OW I UNDERSTAND why Henry VIII
set up his own church."

*—JOHN F. KENNEDY, 1960, AFTER RECEIVING A NOTE
FROM THE VATICAN THAT EXPRESSED CONCERN OVER HIS
POSITION ON THE SEPARATION OF CHURCH AND STATE*

"**K**EEPING UP with Governor Brown's
promises is like trying to read *Playboy* magazine
while your wife turns the pages."

*—RONALD REAGAN, 1966, ON CALIFORNIA
GOVERNOR PAT BROWN*

"**H**ARRISON COMES IN upon a hurricane; God grant
he may not go out upon a wreck."

*—JOHN QUINCY ADAMS, 1840,
ON WILLIAM HENRY HARRISON*

"**W**HY DON'T YOU try to get together ten or fifteen
responsible reporters—if there are that many."

—JIMMY CARTER, ON THE MEDIA

Smiling Cows

FORMER PRESIDENT Calvin Coolidge visited the White House shortly after President Hoover undertook a number of steps aimed at combating the Depression. The much-maligned Hoover described his efforts to his predecessor and expressed his chagrin at both his lack of success and at the amount of criticism aimed at him.

"You can't expect to see calves running in the field," Coolidge pointed out, "the day after you put the bull to the cows."

"No," Hoover replied smartly, "but I would expect to see contented cows."

The Spoils of War

FUTURE PRESIDENTS Rutherford B. Hayes and William McKinley served together in the 23rd Ohio Volunteer Regiment during the Civil War. When the unit was assembled at Ohio's Camp Chase to receive their muskets, the soldiers were indignant about the poor quality and age of the weapons. Excited by the prospect of going off to war, the young Ohioans wanted only the shiniest and best equipment available and refused to accept the worn-out guns. "None of us knew how to use any kind of a musket at that time," McKinley later recalled, "but we thought we knew our rights and we were all conscious of our importance."

Major Hayes addressed the troops and electrified them with his spirit. In a rousing speech, the 39-year-old Hayes challenged the patriotism of the soldiers, reminding them that their forefathers had defeated the British in the Revolution with even cruder weapons. Who were they to spurn their country for the lack of first-class muskets when those who had gone before them had given their very lives for their freedom? The 18-year-old McKinley and his comrades were convinced.

Years later, in an 1893 address at Ohio Wesleyan University, McKinley recalled, "That was our first and last mutiny. We accepted the old-fashioned guns, took what was offered us cheerfully, and Hayes held us captive from that hour. From that moment he had our respect and admiration, which never weakened, but increased during the four eventful years that followed."

Hayes eventually rose to the rank of brigadier general, surviving several wounds to become president in 1877. McKinley followed his former superior officer into the White House 20 years later.

"SOME PEOPLE SAY our speaker might be president in 1960, but, frankly, I don't see why he should take a demotion."
—*JOHN F. KENNEDY, 1959, ON LYNDON JOHNSON, WHOSE POWERFUL INFLUENCE IN THE SENATE WAS WELL KNOWN*

"I HAVE ENDURED a great deal of ridicule without much malice; and have received a great deal of kindness, not quite free from ridicule."
—*ABRAHAM LINCOLN, 1863*

"IT WILL TAKE more than abusive statements to
beat Mr. Nixon—those he can read riding in the
1961 inaugural parade."
—*JOHN F. KENNEDY, 1957, ON RICHARD NIXON*

"DON'T SUPPOSE that because a man is handsome
and dashing that he is a leader. [It's] possible some
little, ornery, measly looking chap you wouldn't look
at twice if you met him in the street may be a leader."
—*WOODROW WILSON, 1910*

Come on In

ON A SPRING DAY in April 1962, nuclear scientist Linus Pauling marched in a ban-the-bomb rally outside the White House. At the march's conclusion Pauling went to his hotel, donned a tuxedo, and returned to the White House, where he was one of 49 Nobel Prize winners scheduled to be honored at a dinner that evening. Aware of his guest's afternoon activities, President John F. Kennedy greeted Pauling by saying, "I'm glad you decided to come inside."

"**I** BELIEVE THE CONSTITUTION is not a salt water animal. . . . It can live as well in fresh as in salt water."

—*MILLARD FILLMORE, RESPONDING SARCASTICALLY TO PRESIDENT POLK'S VETO OF A PLAN FOR RIVER AND HARBOR IMPROVEMENT IN THE GREAT LAKES AREA IN 1846*

"**I** AM ALREADY TIRED of talking about myself."

—*THOMAS JEFFERSON, COMMENTING ON THE PROGRESS OF HIS AUTOBIOGRAPHY, WHICH HE NEVER COMPLETED*

The Matchmaker

As a senator from Tennessee and a presidential candidate in 1824, Andrew Jackson set out from Washington for Nashville, Tennessee, accompanied by Congressman Richard K. Call. Jackson had known Call since the War of 1812, when Call had served as an aide-de-camp to the general during the New Orleans campaign. At that time, Call fell in love with a woman named Mary Kirkland. Unfortunately, Mary's mother forbade her marriage to him because she felt that his connection to General Jackson clashed with her own loyalty to her deceased husband, who had once argued with Jackson over land speculation. Subsequently, Jackson advised the young couple either to part or to elope. They chose the former option but remained in each other's thoughts.

When Jackson and Call reached Nashville in 1824, Jackson resurrected his role of matchmaker in the affair. He again attempted to gain Mrs. Kirkland's blessing for the marriage of her daughter to his colleague, but when she refused this time, the couple finally wed anyway. In anger, Mrs. Kirkland threatened to cut her daughter off from any financial inheritance and sent a pile of letters she had exchanged with Jackson to the *National Gazette* with the intent of ruining his presidential chances. In a final attempt to change her mind, Senator Jackson went to Mrs. Kirkland's home to speak with her in person. He was greeted with hostility, and Mrs. Kirkland ordered him off her property. Jackson refused to leave, saying, "Not until I have had my say."

Not about to give in, the determined woman pulled out a pistol and leveled it at Jackson, again ordering him off the property.

The war hero, who had been involved in his share of duels over the years, stared unflinchingly into Mrs. Kirkland's eyes. Finally, struck either by reason or the futility of his efforts, he gave in. "As you are a woman I will go," he said. "But if you were a man I would not."

"I THINK THIS is the most extraordinary collection of human talent, of human knowledge, that has ever been gathered at the White House—with the possible exception of when Thomas Jefferson dined alone."

—*JOHN F. KENNEDY, 1962*

"I KNOW I'VE GOT a heart big enough to be president.
I know I've got guts enough to be president. But
I wonder whether I've got intelligence and ability
enough to be president—I wonder if any man does?"
—LYNDON BAINES JOHNSON

"HE'LL SIT RIGHT HERE and he'll say do this, do
that! And nothing will happen. Poor Ike—it won't
be a bit like the army."
—HARRY S TRUMAN, 1952, ON GENERAL DWIGHT D.
EISENHOWER'S UPCOMING PRESIDENCY

The Silk Hat

THE TRANSFER of power from Herbert Hoover to Franklin Roosevelt following the 1932 election was hardly amicable. Their differing views on economic policy, together with Roosevelt's landslide victory, brought about cold feelings that lingered for many years between the two. When Roosevelt ran for reelection four years later, he wrote a humorous little parable, which he used to combat attacks on his campaign from the wealthy. In the story, an old man wearing a silk hat fell off a pier, only to be rescued by a friend. The gentleman thanked his rescuer but later criticized him for losing his silk hat.

Upon hearing this story, Hoover spoke up to remind his political foe that someone must first have pushed the old man off the pier.

"I THOUGHT THAT REMARK accusing me of having amnesia was uncalled for. I just wish I could remember who said it."

—RONALD REAGAN, RESPONDING TO WALTER MONDALE'S COMMENT THAT HE RAN "GOVERNMENT BY AMNESIA"

A Royal Gentleman

ANDREW JACKSON'S reputation as a general and a "savage" frontiersman preceded him to Washington. His gentlemanly bearing, however, surprised and won over many people "whose minds were prepared to see me with a Tomahawk in one hand and a scalping knife in the other."

In 1834, future president James Buchanan called on Jackson at the White House with a female, English acquaintance of his. As his friend waited, Buchanan went to Jackson's quarters, where he found the president relaxing before a fire, unshaven and dressed in his robe and slippers. Buchanan made his intention to present the lady known, and "Old Hickory" said he would be happy to meet her. Taken aback by Jackson's apparent intention to greet the woman in such a sloppy state, Buchanan asked if the president planned to change first. Jackson stood up, shook the ashes from his corncob pipe, and replied, "Buchanan, I want to give you a little piece of advice, which I hope you will remember. I knew a man once who made his fortune by attending to his own business. Tell the lady I will see her presently."

Feeling somewhat humiliated, Buchanan retreated to the waiting room to wait for the president. Jackson appeared soon after, dressed in a fine black suit, freshly shaved, with his shock of white hair combed back, and greeted the young lady with the utmost grace. As they left the White House a short time later, the woman turned to Buchanan and said, "Your republican president is the royal model of a gentleman."

"ULYSSES S. GRANT'S period in office seems to prove the theory that we can coast along for eight years without a president. Of course, we've also recently done it with Eisenhower."

—*HARRY S TRUMAN*

"I GET A LITTLE IRRITATED with that constant refrain about compassion. I got an unsigned valentine in February and I'm sure it was from Fritz Mondale. The heart on it was bleeding."

—*RONALD REAGAN, 1983, ON DEMOCRAT WALTER MONDALE*

Views from the Top

"**I**F YOU ARE cast on a desert island
with only a screwdriver, a hatchet,
and a chisel to make a boat with,
why, go make the best one you can.
So with men."

—TEDDY ROOSEVELT, ON HIS EARLY
DEALINGS WITH FELLOW POLITICIANS

"IT IS A GREAT advantage to a president, and a major source of safety to the country, for him to know that he is not a great man."
—CALVIN COOLIDGE, 1929

"THIS NATION cannot afford to be materially rich and spiritually poor."
—JOHN F. KENNEDY, 1963

"WHEN WE GET piled upon one another in large cities as in Europe, we shall become corrupt as in Europe, and go to eating one another as they do there."
—THOMAS JEFFERSON, FROM A 1787 LETTER TO JAMES MADISON

"THE HAPPINESS of society is the end of government."
—JOHN ADAMS, 1776

Trademark Confidence

ACTOR GREGORY PECK remembered waiting by a harbor as a young boy to see President Franklin Roosevelt arrive by boat. A bout with polio had left Roosevelt unable to walk on his own, a fact well guarded by the press, who maintained a sort of silent agreement not to photograph the president in his wheelchair or with his leg braces on. Consequently, few Americans knew the extent of the president's handicap.

As young Peck saw the apparently helpless Roosevelt lifted from the boat upon reaching the shore, he was shocked into tears. After the president was seated on land, however, his disarming smile radiated as he waved to the crowd. Peck quickly forgot his initial impression of Roosevelt's condition. "I started clapping and everything was fine," he later recalled. Roosevelt's trademark confidence could work wonders.

"ONE CANNOT PAY the price of self-respect."
—WOODROW WILSON, 1916

"THERE IS no force so democratic as the force
of an ideal."
—CALVIN COOLIDGE, 1920

"THERE ARE no good laws but such as
repeal other laws."
—ANDREW JOHNSON, 1835

"EAT PLENTY, wisely, without waste."
—HERBERT HOOVER, ADVISING THE NATION, 1917

What Do You Mean by That?

MARTIN VAN BUREN earned the monikers "The Little Magician" and "The Red Fox of Kinderhook" for his political adroitness and skill at keeping his thoughts close to his vest. The clever politician seldom revealed his position on any matter unless he was completely sure of himself. This policy was often put to the test. For instance, a senator once bet a colleague that he could trap Van Buren into committing to an opinion.

"Matt," he asked, "it's been rumored that the sun rises in the East. Do you believe it?"

"Well, Senator," the wily Van Buren answered, "I understand that's the common acceptance, but as I never get up till after dawn I can't really say."

On another occasion, a reporter approached Van Buren aboard a steamer on the Hudson River. "Fine day, isn't it, Mr. Van Buren?"

Not to be caught so easily, Van Buren replied, "Now that depends on what you mean by a fine day. There are all sorts of fine days. This particular one…"

Silent Cal

THOUGH HE POSSESSED a clever mind and a dry wit, Calvin Coolidge generally lived up to his nickname, "Silent Cal." He followed his own maxim that he could do himself no harm by saying nothing. He once asked an associate to visit him at his office. The gentleman remained for more than a half hour without a word passing between the two men. When he finally got up to leave, Coolidge said, "Thank you for coming. I wanted to think."

"YOU CAN FOOL some of the people all of the time, and all of the people some of the time, but you can't fool all of the people all of the time."

—ABRAHAM LINCOLN, 1856

"A MAN who has never lost himself in a cause bigger than himself has missed one of life's mountaintop experiences."

—RICHARD NIXON, 1968

"**E**VERY DIFFERENCE of opinion is not a difference of principle."

—*THOMAS JEFFERSON, IN HIS FIRST INAUGURAL ADDRESS, 1801*

"**G**RIEF DRIVES men into habits of serious reflection, sharpens the understanding, and softens the heart."

—*JOHN ADAMS, 1816*

"**A**LL I WANT them to say about me is what they said about John Adams, 'He kept the peace.'"

—*JOHN F. KENNEDY*

"**W**E HAVE FOUND that it is easier for men to die together on the field of battle than it is for them to live together at home in peace."

—*HARRY S TRUMAN, 1946*

An Order's an Order

ULYSSES S. GRANT, commander of all Union armies by 1864, rose to his high station from the insignificant prewar position of clerk in a leather goods shop. Grant never became too haughty to forget his modest past. At his headquarters at City Point, Virginia, in 1864, General Grant issued an order designed to prevent any chance of fire. One day, as he walked across a newly constructed wooden wharf with a lit cigar in his mouth, a soldier called out, "It's against orders to come on the wharf with a lighted cigar." Grant immediately threw the cigar into the river and said, "I don't like to lose my smoke, but the sentinel's right. He evidently isn't going to let me disobey my own orders."

"THIS ISN'T the way they told me it was when I first decided to run for the presidency. After reading about the schedules of the president, I thought we all stayed in bed until ten or eleven and then got out and drove around."

—JOHN F. KENNEDY, 1960

"WHEREVER THE STANDARD of freedom
and independence has been unfurled, there will
[America's] heart, her benedictions,
and her prayers be."
—*JOHN QUINCY ADAMS, 1821*

"IF A MAN permits largeness of heart to degenerate
into softness of head he inevitably becomes a
nuisance in any relation of life."
—*THEODORE ROOSEVELT*

Role Reversal

ZACHARY TAYLOR could hardly have been described as dashing or well-dressed. He often appeared unkempt, even sloppy. He eschewed formality and earned the nickname "Old Rough and Ready" by his willingness to share soldiers' privations while he was an officer in the Seminole Wars.

Another future president, Ulysses S. Grant, served under Taylor during the Mexican War and could remember only two instances when General Taylor actually wore his uniform in the field. On one of these occasions, Taylor was to meet with the flag officer of an American naval squadron. Knowing the Navy's propensity for dressing to the hilt on formal occasions, Taylor thought it would be proper for him to wear his full uniform. Meanwhile, the naval officer, aware of Taylor's habit of wearing plain clothing rather than military garb, deliberately left his uniform behind. The meeting, Grant later recalled, "was said to have been embarrassing to both, and the conversation was principally apologetic."

"**A**LL RIGHT. You deserve to be shot as much as anybody. You shall go."

—*THEODORE ROOSEVELT, 1898, TO A PLEADING "ROUGH RIDER" HE HAD PLANNED TO LEAVE OUT OF THE INVASION OF CUBA DURING THE SPANISH-AMERICAN WAR. THE SOLDIER HAD BEEN A DISCIPLINE PROBLEM IN CAMP.*

"**W**HEN ANGRY, count ten before you speak; if very angry, a hundred."

—*THOMAS JEFFERSON, 1825*

"**A** MOCKINGBIRD IMITATES robins, jays, redbirds, crows, hawks—but has no individual note of his own. A lot of people [are] like that."

—*HARRY S TRUMAN, 1948. TRUMAN WROTE THIS ON A SCRAP OF PAPER AS HE SAT ON THE WHITE HOUSE'S SOUTH PORCH LOOKING OUT OVER THE PROPERTY.*

"**H**E SAID he was against it."

—*CALVIN COOLIDGE, EXPLAINING WHAT A CLERGYMAN PREACHING ABOUT SIN HAD SAID*

"FELLOW CITIZENS, we cannot escape history.
We . . . will be remembered in spite of ourselves."
—*ABRAHAM LINCOLN, 1862*

"THE BASIS OF our government being the opinion
of the people, the very first object should be to keep
that right; and were it left to me to decide whether
we should have a government without newspapers,
or newspapers without a government, I should not
hesitate a moment to prefer the latter."
—*THOMAS JEFFERSON, 1787*

Penny Pincher

FROM HIS YOUTH, James Buchanan meticulously tracked his expenditures and income—practically to the last penny—and kept it all on record in notebooks. Buchanan's personal estate was valued at up to $200,000, yet he continued to track the pettiest expenses. On one occasion, he returned a $15,000 check given him by a friend because of a 10-cent error in it. While president, Buchanan once accidentally paid three cents too little for an order of food for the White House. The merchant ignored the petty error, but when Buchanan discovered it he immediately forwarded the three pennies, explaining that he expected to pay neither too much nor too little, but exactly what he owed.

"I WOULD PREFER to go into the war if I knew I was to die or be killed in the course of it, than to live through and after it without taking any part in it."

—RUTHERFORD B. HAYES, ON THE CIVIL WAR. HAYES EVENTUALLY ROSE TO THE RANK OF BREVET MAJOR GENERAL IN THE UNION ARMY.

The Battle of New Orleans

As BRITISH FORCES approached New Orleans in December 1814 during the War of 1812, General Andrew Jackson found it necessary to impose martial law in order to gain control of the city he was trying to defend. In protest of this act, a federal district judge named Domick Augustine Hall issued a writ of habeas corpus to free a legislator whom Jackson had jailed for writing an article critical of the general's policies. Jackson responded by throwing the judge into the same cell as the legislator.

When news of the official end of the war reached New Orleans in March, Jackson finally ended martial law. Judge Hall returned to his seat on the court and immediately ordered the general to appear and explain why he should not be held in contempt. On March 24, 1815, the United States *v.* Major General Andrew Jackson trial opened. Jackson appeared with a prepared statement to explain why the charge against him should be dropped, but Hall refused to allow it. The judge found Jackson guilty and fined him $1,000.

Jackson's many supporters took up a collection and easily raised the sum, but the general refused the money. He had had no desire to break the law and considered himself, like everyone else, responsible for his own actions. He paid the fine himself and directed that the collected funds be used to help the families of American soldiers who had died in the Battle of New Orleans.

Many New Orleans residents remained angry with Jackson. The Louisiana Senate, in fact, deliberately omitted Jackson's name from its list of officers whom it thanked for saving the city.

"THERE IS ONLY one form of political strategy in which I have any confidence, and that is to try to do the right thing and sometimes be able to succeed."
—CALVIN COOLIDGE, 1929

"IN MY MASHED POTATO tours, I have said many times that government doesn't tax to get the money it needs, government always finds a need for the money it gets."
—RONALD REAGAN

"A MAN WHO HAS never gone to school may steal from a freight car; but if he has a university education, he may steal the whole railroad."

—THEODORE ROOSEVELT

"IT IS WONDERFUL how much may be done if we are always doing."

—THOMAS JEFFERSON, 1787

"IF THE RABBLE were lopped off at one end and the aristocrat at the other, all would be well with the country."

—ANDREW JOHNSON

"I WONDER WHY we are made so that what we really think and feel we cover up?"

—HARRY S TRUMAN, FROM AN UNSENT,
1945 LETTER TO HIS WIFE, BESS

The Fine Art of Negotiating

DWIGHT D. EISENHOWER learned a valuable lesson when he was just four years old. After watching some geese at play outside his house one day, curiosity got the best of him. The youngster approached a goose, whose male partner chased little Dwight back into the house. Unwilling to admit defeat, Eisenhower continued to venture outside, only to be sent running again and again by the defiant gander. Finally, armed by his uncle with a cut-down broom handle, Dwight sought out his enemy, and with a shout and a swing of his weapon, sent the alarmed gander fleeing. From then on, Dwight ruled the yard. As he recounted later, the quasi-war taught him "never to negotiate with an adversary except from a position of strength."

"**I** AM for economy—and then more economy."
—CALVIN COOLIDGE

"**B**USINESS IS all right so long as it is not sordid, and it cannot be sordid if it is shot through with ideals."
—WOODROW WILSON, 1916

The Power of a Good Laugh

"**I** LAUGH BECAUSE I must not weep," Abraham Lincoln once said. The warm-hearted president loved to tell a good joke, and his prolific use of folksy humor endeared him to Americans. Lincoln, much like John F. Kennedy a century later, understood how a little humor can calm troubled minds. The president eased the tension of a September 22, 1862, cabinet meeting by reading aloud from a book by his favorite humorist, Artemus Ward. Having produced a few smiles from his subordinates, the president turned quietly serious and unveiled his Emancipation Proclamation. His cabinet quickly approved it.

"**I** HAVE GIVEN UP newspapers in exchange for Tacitus and Thucydides, for Newton and Euclid, and I find myself much the happier."
—*THOMAS JEFFERSON, 1812*

"**N**OW, a woman has a perfect right to talk temperance . . . but her right to wear pants and make the night hideous on the street is questioned."
—*WARREN G. HARDING*

"**I** THINK probably politicians are about half ego and half humility. I think I have my share of both of them."
—*JIMMY CARTER, 1975*

"**I**F YOU DON'T ever fall on your face, you forget how hard life is for a lot of people all the time."
—*BILL CLINTON*

The Price of Asparagus

DURING WORLD WAR II, Franklin Roosevelt often consulted with friends and colleagues and occasionally visited factories and other war production facilities to try to keep abreast of popular opinion. His physical condition, however, made it impossible for him to get out and speak to people as much as he liked.

In 1943, Roosevelt entertained skeptical reporters with the story of a discussion he had supposedly had with a mechanic, who had complained to the president about the price of asparagus. According to the president, he asked the man if he'd ever eaten asparagus in March before. The vegetable, Roosevelt said, had been shipped from Florida, a seemingly trivial kind of benefit that Americans seemed not to notice. "You know, I never thought of that. I will have to talk to my wife about it," the man said thoughtfully. The point of Roosevelt's anecdote was simply to explain that his economic programs were necessary for keeping inflation low.

At a press conference one year later, the president introduced the same topic during a discussion about economics. In this version of the story, the mechanic was replaced by a foreman. The foreman complained of the high cost of living; in particular, the "dollar and a quarter" price of asparagus. At that point, an Associated Press correspondent interrupted the president: "Mr. President, is that the same foreman . . . ?" The room erupted in laughter, with Roosevelt joining in.

Reporters wondered with some amusement and skepticism at the apparent ease with which mechanics and other folks could supposedly drop in on the president. Strangely enough, however, an economist recalled years later how he had entered Roosevelt's office one day to find him talking earnestly with a workman about the high cost of asparagus.

"I FIND THE PAIN of a little censure, even when it is unfounded, is more acute than the pleasure of much praise."

—THOMAS JEFFERSON, 1789

"**B**ETTER [TO] GIVE your path to a dog, than be bitten by him in contesting the right."

—*ABRAHAM LINCOLN*

"**W**HEN MORE and more people are thrown out of work, unemployment results."

—*CALVIN COOLIDGE*

"**I** LIKE the dreams of the future better than the history of the past."

—*THOMAS JEFFERSON, 1816*

"**B**ETTER A THOUSAND TIMES to go down fighting than to dip your colors to dishonorable compromise."

—*WOODROW WILSON*

The Edge of the Chart

JOURNALIST GEORGE CREEL once compared Herbert Hoover to "a stretch of blank wall," and said that writing about Hoover was "like trying to describe the interior of a citadel where every drawbridge is up and every portcullis down." In private, however, Hoover could be spontaneously witty.

During the Depression, as he examined a chart on the wall of his office indicating a stock's value spiraling downward, he was asked, "What if the stock's value drops another ten points?"

"It can't," Hoover replied dryly, pointing to the chart, "there's the edge of the chart."

"MY LOVE OF FUN is so great, and my perception of the ludicrous so quick, that I laugh at everything witty, and say all I can to add to the general mirth. Now this [is] agreeable enough at times, but the tendency to carry it to extremes is so great that I shall stop it entirely in future, if I can."

—*RUTHERFORD B. HAYES, AGE 18, FROM AN 1841 DIARY ENTRY*

Learn to Box!

ONE DAY DURING the 1964 presidential campaign, Jimmy Carter's son Chip wore an LBJ pin to school in support of Democratic candidate Lyndon Johnson. His political sympathies went unappreciated by some anti-Johnson students, who ripped it from his shirt. Chip buttoned it back on, and again it was torn off. After a few days of this back-and-forth dispute, a group of kids not only removed his pin but also roughed Chip up pretty well. Angry and smarting from his thrashing, Chip returned home in tears and sought his father's advice. Carter instructed young Chip to put the pin back on.

"What if they tear it off again?" Chip asked his father.

"Then you just put it back on again if you want to wear it," Carter told his son. "Do what you want to do—and learn to box."

"TOWERING GENIUS disdains a beaten path. It seeks regions hitherto unexplored."
—*ABRAHAM LINCOLN, 1838*

"I NEVER SAW an instance of one of two disputants convincing the other by argument."
—*THOMAS JEFFERSON, 1798*

"WHEN I DIE I desire no better winding sheet than the Stars and Stripes, and no softer pillow than the Constitution of my country."
—*ANDREW JOHNSON*

"IT HAS BEEN my observation in life that, if one will only exercise the patience to wait, his wants are likely to be filled."
—*CALVIN COOLIDGE*

"MY POLITICS are short and sweet, like the old woman's dance."

—*ABRAHAM LINCOLN, 1832*

"THERE'S AN OLD saying down in Texas, if you know you are right, just keep coming on and no gun can stop you."

—*LYNDON JOHNSON*

Did You Get All That?

NO BETTER EXAMPLE of Calvin Coolidge's propensity for silence exists than his manner of dictating speeches. His stenographer's patience and resolve were tested often. On more than one occasion, the notetaker sat all night, with pencil and pad in hand, without hearing the president utter a single word for him to copy. After mulling his thoughts for hours while his aide grew stiff from sitting, Coolidge would sometimes suddenly say, "That is all. You may come back at eight o'clock in the morning."

Financial Faux Pas

PRESIDENT WILLIAM HOWARD TAFT was known for his big heart and kindly nature. He was unfamiliar with the art of the politician, however, and often blurted out comments that got him into trouble and made his supporters cringe. He once caused stock prices to plunge when, in a speech to a group of college students, he mentioned offhandedly, "within the next decade there will be some reaction or some financial stringency," or "perhaps a financial panic."

Most people realized that Taft's political blunders were simply the result of his not knowing any better. Iowa's Henry C. Wallace once wrote that if "you put Taft and a trap in a section of land in the night and wanted to find him, you would simply need to go to that part of the square mile where the trap was located and you would find him in it."

Domestic
Policies

"**I** AM THE MAN who accompanied Jacqueline
Kennedy to Paris, and I have enjoyed it."

—JOHN F. KENNEDY, 1961. THE FIRST LADY
WAS EXTREMELY POPULAR IN FRANCE.

An Embarrassing Encounter

MARK TWAIN'S FIRST INTRODUCTION to President Ulysses S. Grant proved awkward. After shaking hands with the grim-faced president, Twain stood silent for a long moment before saying, "Mr. President, I am embarrassed. Are you?"

Ten years later, the two met again. A similar silence followed their initial greeting, until the tight-lipped Grant finally said, "I am not embarrassed, are you?"

"**O**UR FAMILY didn't exactly come from the wrong side of the tracks, but we were certainly always within sound of the train whistles."

—*RONALD REAGAN*

"**T**HERE IS no dignity quite so impressive, and no independence quite so important, as living within your means."

—*CALVIN COOLIDGE, 1929*

"**N**OTHING NEW HERE, except my marrying, which to me, is a matter of profound wonder."

—*ABRAHAM LINCOLN, 1842*

"**I** HAD NOT the advantage of a classical education, and no man should, in my judgment, accept a degree he cannot read."

—*MILLARD FILLMORE, ON DECLINING TO ACCEPT AN HONORARY DEGREE FROM THE UNIVERSITY OF OXFORD IN 1855*

"**A**BSTRACTED from home, I know no happiness in this world."

—*THOMAS JEFFERSON, 1780*

"**M**y wife and I had an argument for fourteen years...which I finally won."

—*JIMMY CARTER, 1976, ON THE AGE DIFFERENCE BETWEEN HIS OLDER SONS AND YOUNG DAUGHTER*

"**I**T IS EASY to make acquaintances, but very difficult to shake them off, however irksome and unprofitable they are found after we have once committed ourselves to them."
—*GEORGE WASHINGTON*

"**I**N LIFE, as in a football game, the principle to follow is: Hit the line hard; don't foul and don't shirk, but hit the line hard."
—*THEODORE ROOSEVELT*

"**A** GOOD MANY things go around in the dark besides Santa Claus."
—*HERBERT HOOVER, 1935*

"**L**ABOR DISGRACES no man; unfortunately you occasionally find men disgrace labor."
—*ULYSSES S. GRANT, 1877*

And You Are . . . ?

GEORGE BUSH WAS ONCE talking to a group of people when a woman approached him and said, "Peter, how are you?" and began talking to the astounded president. Realizing that she had him confused with someone else, Bush said politely, "I'm George Bush, the President of the United States." The woman was embarrassed, and Bush felt sorry for her. Some time later he sent her a photograph of himself with his dog, Ranger, noting on it, "I enjoyed meeting you. I'm the one on the left."

"The President"

JOHN QUINCY ADAMS WAS particularly ill-tempered in his later years. He was usually referred to by family members as "the president," rather than the traditional "grandpa" or other warm title. Adams's grandson Henry, however, later recalled an incident from his youth that altered his impression of his grandfather and helped forge a bond of respect between them.

One summer day when Henry was six or seven years old, he decided he didn't want to go to school. As he stood at the foot of a staircase leading to the former president's library, vehemently resisting his mother's wishes, Henry was more than holding his own when the library door swung open and old Grandfather Adams emerged. Without saying a word, "the president" put on his hat, walked down the stairs, took Henry by the hand, and led him outside and up the road toward town. As the astounded youngster walked, he thought about how unlikely it was that a man nearing 80 would consider walking so far in the summer sun. Suddenly he found himself seated in the schoolhouse; only then did old Mr. Adams release his grandson's hand and depart, leaving Henry to ponder how he had been so thoroughly defeated in his bid for a day out of school.

"**I** TOLD HIM that Mrs. Carter and I would be deeply hurt and shocked and disappointed . . . because our daughter is only seven years old."

—*JIMMY CARTER, 1975, RELATING HOW A REPORTER HAD ASKED HIM HOW HE WOULD FEEL IF HIS DAUGHTER HAD A PREMARITAL AFFAIR*

"**H**APPINESS LIES not in the mere possession of money; it lies in the joy of achievement, in the thrill of creative effort."

—*FRANKLIN D. ROOSEVELT, IN HIS FIRST INAUGURAL ADDRESS, 1933*

"**I** HAVE NOW come to the conclusion never again to think of marrying, and for this reason: I can never be satisfied with anyone who would be blockhead enough to have me."

—*ABRAHAM LINCOLN, 1838*

"**I** CAN DO ONE of two things. I can be
President of the United States or I can control Alice.
I cannot possibly do both."
—*TEDDY ROOSEVELT, ON HIS DAUGHTER, ALICE*

"**T**HE LADY BEARER of this says she has
two sons who want to work. Set them at it if
possible. Wanting to work is so rare a want
that it should be encouraged."
—*ABRAHAM LINCOLN, 1861, ON A MOTHER'S
REQUEST FOR WORK FOR HER SONS*

Bygones

MARTIN VAN BUREN WAS NOT the type to make quick, rash decisions. He was, in fact, a calculated thinker well known for remaining silent on a subject until he was absolutely secure in his position. When he made a decision, however, he stuck by it without regard for consequences. As a young lawyer in 1811, Van Buren exchanged insults with an impetuous political foe named John Sudam, who subsequently challenged Van Buren to a duel. Though he opposed the practice, Van Buren would not think of declining the "invitation." He aggressively made preparations for the showdown. After his foe haggled over the arrangement, however, the duel was put off and Van Buren denounced his enemy as a coward.

The two remained cold toward each other for years. One day they found themselves seated opposite one another in a tavern. Sudam awkwardly asked his longtime opponent to pass a bottle of wine. Van Buren, his better nature winning out, instead asked Sudam to share a glass with him. With that, the feud ended, and the two strolled together from the tavern arm in arm.

Federal Disaster Relief

PRESIDENT REAGAN ONCE RECEIVED a letter from a South Carolina boy requesting federal disaster relief funds. Reagan penned him a lighthearted, wry response in which he pointed out that resources were extremely limited due to an abundance of disasters that year: countless hurricanes, floods, earthquakes, drought, and forest fires. "I'm sure your mother was fully justified in proclaiming your room a disaster," the president wrote, and suggested that the boy follow the example of the administration's new Private Sector Initiatives Program, which advocated volunteerism in the solving of local problems.

"I AM IN NO HURRY about having my boys learn to write. I would much prefer that they would lay up a stock of health by knocking about the country than to hear that they were the best scholars of their age in Ohio."

—RUTHERFORD B. HAYES

"THERE IS the politician of the family. If she had only let me alone I should now be dozing on the Circuit Court Bench."

—*WILLIAM HOWARD TAFT, REFERRING TO HIS WIFE, NELLIE*

"I NEVER WAR against females, and it is only the base and cowardly that do."

—*ANDREW JACKSON, 1827*

"I HAVE FOUND the best way to give advice to your children is to find out what they want and then advise them to do it."

—*HARRY S TRUMAN, 1955*

"THE FACT that our children still come home."

—*GEORGE BUSH, ON THE SINGLE ACCOMPLISHMENT OF WHICH HE WAS MOST PROUD*

"**I** SEE NOTHING wrong with giving Robert some legal experience as Attorney General before he goes out to practice law."

—*JOHN F. KENNEDY, 1961, ON NAMING HIS BROTHER U.S. ATTORNEY GENERAL*

"**H**ER BROTHERS are so much older that it is almost as though she has four fathers and we have had to stand in line to spoil her."

—*JIMMY CARTER, ON HIS DAUGHTER, AMY*

"**I** WOULD rather be in bed."

—*JAMES MADISON, 1809, AT THE INAUGURAL BALL, AT WHICH HE WAS UPSTAGED BY HIS ATTRACTIVE AND VIVACIOUS WIFE, DOLLY*

"**N**EVER DO ANYTHING or say anything that you would be ashamed to confide to your mother."

—*RUTHERFORD B. HAYES, TO HIS SONS*

Tickling the Ivories

HARRY TRUMAN LOVED to play the piano and had once dreamed of becoming a concert pianist. His affinity for tickling the ivories, however, got him into hot water in early 1945. While playing piano in a stage show for servicemen at the Washington Press Club canteen, Truman was delighted when Lauren Bacall was suddenly lifted atop his piano. The soldiers cheered wildly, flashbulbs popped, and Truman grinned broadly as the actress struck a seductive pose. The resulting photographs of the impromptu session perturbed some who thought Truman had perhaps enjoyed himself too much. An indignant Bess Truman agreed, and suggested to Harry that he should stop playing the piano in public.

A Good Man

BEHIND PRESIDENT HERBERT HOOVER'S straight-laced image was a man of private emotion whose compassion for those in need was profound. Those who worked closely with him recognized this, but the president shielded this side of himself from the public.

One day in 1932, three children showed up at the White House after hitchhiking all the way from Detroit. Their unemployed father, Charles Feagan, had been searching for work and had been arrested on a charge of auto theft. The children, led by 13-year-old Bernice, had come to the capital hoping the president could help their father.

Hoover was impressed by the youngsters' determination. He told his secretary, Theodore G. Joslin, that "three children resourceful enough to get to Washington to see me are going to see me." Joslin led the kids into Hoover's office and scrambled to find details on the case. The president smiled warmly and shook the hands of the nervous children. He asked them their names, then turned to Bernice and asked her to tell him their story. Shy in the presence of the president, Bernice talked haltingly at first but grew more comfortable as Hoover listened patiently. The details of her account matched largely with the reports Joslin received, and the president reassured her that he was making an inquiry into the case.

"I know there must be good in a man whose children are so well behaved and who show such loyalty and devotion to him," Hoover told Bernice warmly. "I will use my good offices. You may go home happy." Hoover gave each child a small memento and sent them on their way home. "Dad will be waiting there for you," he added.

Mr. Joslin entered the president's office a moment later to find Hoover staring silently out the window. Without turning around, Hoover said, "Get that father out of jail immediately." Hoover refused to allow the incident any more publicity than a slight announcement. "That is all we will say about it," he said. "Now we will get back to work."

"**M**Y FATHER was not a failure. After all, he was the father of a President of the United States."

—*HARRY S TRUMAN, IN RESPONSE TO A COMMENT THAT HIS FATHER, JOHN ANDERSON TRUMAN, HAD BEEN A FAILURE*

"**I** WAS the Errol Flynn of the B's."

—*RONALD REAGAN, ON HIS ACTING CAREER*

"**M**OM, aren't the kids in Arkansas born with the same brain as people [in other states]?"

—*BILL CLINTON, AGE 8 OR 9, AFTER READING A NEWSPAPER ARTICLE ABOUT ARKANSAS' RATINGS IN NATIONAL EDUCATION SURVEYS*

"**M**RS. MONROE HATH added a daughter to our society who, though noisy, contributes greatly to its amusement."

—*JAMES MONROE, FROM A LETTER
TO THOMAS JEFFERSON*

Teddy Who?

THEODORE ROOSEVELT WAS PERHAPS the most physically active president ever. He loved the outdoors, hunting, and just about every type of exercise. In the White House he was always on the go, hiking, boxing, even learning the art of jujitsu. He sustained bruises playing "single stick" with his former Spanish-American War comrade, General Leonard Wood, and engaged in wrestling matches with Japanese wrestlers at the White House.

Roosevelt's seven-year-old son, Quentin, was once asked about his father's endless activities. "Yes, I see him sometimes," Quentin said, "but I know nothing of his family life."

Dr. Blades

IN 1858, A MAN NAMED Franklin Blades wrote to Abraham Lincoln requesting the use of his name as a reference in his new profession as a lawyer. The two had met a year earlier, during a meeting of Republican members of the Illinois House of Representatives, at which time Blades was a practicing physician. Blades neglected to mention his change of profession in his letter, prompting the following reply from his quick-witted benefactor: "I do not know whether you are Dr. Blades or not. If you are Dr. Blades, you may use my name; if you are not Dr. Blades, if Dr. Blades says you may use my name, you may do so."

"I HAVE READ your lousy review of Margaret's concert. I've come to the conclusion that you are an eight-ulcer man on a four-ulcer job. Someday, I hope to meet you. When that happens, you'll need a new nose, a lot of beefsteak for black eyes, and perhaps a supporter below."

—*HARRY S TRUMAN, 1950, TO CRITIC PAUL HUME, WHO HAD GIVEN THE PRESIDENT'S DAUGHTER'S SINGING A POOR REVIEW*

"**I**T'S LEGAL for you to do this—because I can assure
you there's nothing in here for either of you."
—*JOHN F. KENNEDY, 1954, TO AIDES WHO WERE
SERVING AS WITNESSES TO HIS WILL*

"**F**IGHTING BATTLES is like courting girls:
those who make the most pretensions and
are boldest usually win."
—*RUTHERFORD B. HAYES*

"**A**LL MY CHILDREN have spoken for themselves
since they first learned to speak, and not always with
my advance approval. I expect that to continue."
—*GERALD FORD, 1976*

"**T**HE ONLY REASON in this world that I would like
to have a lot of money [is] I believe I know where to
place it. . . . I know where it's needed."
—*BILL CLINTON*

As American as Apple Pie

MRS. CALVIN COOLIDGE's first attempt to bake an apple pie for her husband proved memorable. It did not turn out as well as hoped; it was, in fact, rather tough, and the couple did not eat much of it. Later that same evening, two friends of Mrs. Coolidge dropped by and Calvin saw a chance to do away with the disappointing dessert. The Coolidges watched with contrasting feelings—she with anxiety and he with glee—as the visitors devoured the pie. As they finished, Mr. Coolidge turned to them and said seriously, "Don't you think the road commissioner would be willing to pay my wife something for her recipe for pie crust?"

"**R**OMANCE is like a colt. It must be broken
before it is safe to ride."

—*THOMAS JEFFERSON, 1814*

"**I** SHALL WORRY you so much with my appetite that
you must gain strength to meet the trial."

—*WILLIAM HOWARD TAFT, 1895, TO HIS WIFE. TAFT
TOPPED THE SCALES AT AROUND 350 POUNDS
DURING HIS YEARS IN THE WHITE HOUSE.*

"**I**T'S CHEAPER that way because we can
all use the luggage."

—*LYNDON JOHNSON, ON THE PREPONDERANCE OF THE
INITIALS "LBJ" IN HIS FAMILY. EVEN HIS DOG
WAS NAMED LITTLE BEAGLE JOHNSON.*

"**I** HAVE NO news to give you; for I have none but
the newspapers, and believing little of that myself,
it would be an unworthy present to my friends."

—*THOMAS JEFFERSON, 1820*

Profile in Courage

AS A YOUNG LAWYER in Pennsylvania, James Buchanan built a reputation for cleverness and exceptional skill in arguing cases. He once defended a client who had been charged with threatening the life of another man. When the plaintiff took the stand, Buchanan asked him whether he would have taken much notice of the threat if he had been more courageous.

"I am a man of as much courage as anybody, sir," the plaintiff answered.

"Then you were not frightened when my client threatened you?" asked Buchanan.

"No, sir," came the reply.

"You are not afraid of him?" Buchanan continued.

"No, I am not," answered the defiant plaintiff.

Buchanan then neatly tied up his argument. "Well, then, what did you bring this charge for? I move its dismissal."

The case was dismissed.

"AGAIN, I have been proud of my descent (not very, of course, only a trifle so) from the famous Rutherfords; but it is plain that the brains, energy, and character possessed by my grandfather's children and grandchildren . . . are mainly derived from our plain ancestor—who Uncle Sardis says was the homeliest woman he ever saw— Grandmother Chloe Smith."

—*RUTHERFORD B. HAYES, FROM AN 1870 DIARY ENTRY IN WHICH HE DISCUSSED HIS THOUGHTS ON GENEALOGY*

"SIR, I HAVE BEEN TRYING ever since you went away to learn to write you a letter. I shall make poor work of it, but, sir, Mamma says you will accept my endeavors, and that my duty to you may be expressed in poor writing as well as good. . . . We all long to see you. I am, sir, your dutiful son, John Quincy Adams.

—*JOHN QUINCY ADAMS, AGE 8, FROM A LETTER TO HIS FATHER, JOHN ADAMS*

Where Did I Come From?

LYNDON JOHNSON LIKED to describe to people his rural upbringing, which he sometimes compared to that of Abraham Lincoln. Once, while giving a tour of his LBJ ranch in Texas, he pointed out a beaten-down old cabin and told his listeners it was his birthplace. Johnson's mother was present and later pulled him aside to quietly remind him that he had actually been born in a much nicer house close to town—a house that had since been torn down. "I know, Mama," Johnson responded, "but everybody has to have a birthplace."

"Friendly" Fire

MARTIN VAN BUREN kept to himself, although occasionally he used his notorious reticence to make a point. Once, while the president was receiving guests during a White House function, Henry Clay remarked that it must be nice for him to be surrounded by so many friends. Van Buren, who was politically adept enough to know something about the motives of his many "friends," replied with a touch of cynicism, "Well, the weather is very fine."

"THERE WAS about one human being to
each square mile."
—ABRAHAM LINCOLN, ON HARDIN COUNTY,
KENTUCKY, WHERE HE WAS BORN

"I MEAN TO CALL the little child Esther.
It is a favorite name with me and associated in a
pleasant way with things I remember besides
the hanging of Haman."
—GROVER CLEVELAND, 1893, ON HIS NEWBORN DAUGHTER

The Pursuit
of Happiness

"THE OTHER DAY I gave up my seat in a streetcar and three ladies sat down."

—WILLIAM HOWARD TAFT,
ON HIS OWN GIRTH

Only in America

As a young law student, Andrew Jackson earned
a reputation as "the most roaring, rollicking, game-
cocking, horse-racing, card-playing, mischievous
fellow" who ever lived in Salisbury, North Carolina.
After each day spent working in a law office, Jackson
and some friends would let off steam by getting
drunk or pulling various pranks. Among their
favorite activities were stealing signposts and relocat-
ing outhouses to uncomfortably faraway locations.

One year, when Jackson was asked to arrange
a Christmas ball for a local dancing school he fre-
quented, his penchant for practical jokes got him
in hot water. He sent invitations to the town's most
notorious pair of prostitutes, who showed up at the
ball in their best working clothes and were greeted by
gasps of shock from appalled dancers. The humor of
the prank was lost on everyone but Jackson.

On another occasion, Jackson was enjoying
himself with some friends at a local tavern when they
decided to share in a ritualistic shattering of their
glasses. Throwing them to the floor with great flair,
the boys decided to smash the table as well. The
friends then went all out in celebration, destroying

chairs and a cot, tearing down curtains, and setting the entire mess ablaze. This done, they departed full of cheer. Jackson never forgot that wild evening, and neither did the town's residents.

Years later, when news of Jackson's presidential candidacy reached Salisbury, few could believe that the law student who had spent more time carousing than studying might soon be leading the country. One woman summed up public opinion by exclaiming, "Well, if Andrew Jackson can be president, anybody can."

"IT IS POSSIBLE I may lose my scalp from the temper of the Indians, but if either a little fighting or a great deal of running will save it, I shall escape safe."
—*JAMES MONROE, 1784, ABOUT TO EMBARK ON A FRONTIER TRIP*

"I'M WILLING to leave things alone if you will guarantee that I can go to bed and find them the same in the morning."
—*WOODROW WILSON, 1912*

"**T**HE PITCHING of Lynch of the Nationals was something wonderful, not only in the strength with which he pitched the ball, but in the skill with which he deceived the batsmen."

—*JAMES A. GARFIELD, 1879, COMMENTING ON A "MATCH GAME OF BALL" [BASEBALL GAME] HE ATTENDED. HE QUICKLY BECAME A FAN OF THE SPORT.*

"**I** SMOKED TOBACCO and read Milton at the same time, and from the same motive—to find out what was the recondite charm in them which gave my father so much pleasure. After making myself four or five times sick with smoking, I mastered that accomplishment. . . . But I did not master Milton."

—*JOHN QUINCY ADAMS, FROM AN 1829 DIARY ENTRY*

"**M**Y PREDECESSOR did not object, as I do, to pictures of one's golfing skills in action. But neither, on the other hand, did he ever bean a Secret Service man."

—*JOHN F. KENNEDY*

"**B**UT THOUGH I am an old man, I am but a
young gardener."
—*THOMAS JEFFERSON, 1811*

"**M**Y TIME is being pretty well filled up now,
especially as I insist on taking the whole
afternoon for golf."
—*WILLIAM HOWARD TAFT*

"**P**EOPLE DIE, but books never die."
—*FRANKLIN DELANO ROOSEVELT, 1942*

"**FROM MY EARLIEST** recollection, I have thought I had great power in me, yet at the same time I was fully satisfied of my present insignificance and mental weakness. I have imagined that at some future time I could do considerable, but the more I learn, the more I feel my littleness."

—*RUTHERFORD B. HAYES, AT AGE 19*

"**I AM NOT** a Julius Caesar, nor a Napoleon, but a plain Hoosier colonel, with no more relish for a fight than for a good breakfast and hardly so much."

—*BENJAMIN HARRISON, ON HIS LACK OF TASTE FOR MILITARY LIFE. HARRISON EVENTUALLY ROSE TO THE RANK OF BRIGADIER GENERAL.*

"**I WANT TO GET IN** as much traveling as I can during these four years, for after they are over I do not know when I will get another opportunity."

—*WILLIAM HOWARD TAFT, ON HIS FONDNESS FOR EXCURSIONS FROM THE WHITE HOUSE*

Put It on My Tab

WHEN JAMES BUCHANAN replaced Franklin Pierce as president in 1857, the social atmosphere in the nation's capital brightened considerably. Buchanan was a bachelor who thoroughly enjoyed a good time, and much mention was made of his "resisting power against the fumes of intoxicating drinks." When his supply ran low, Buchanan would sometimes extend his Sunday drive to church to a nearby distillery for a ten-gallon cask of "Old J. B. Whiskey."

Soon after his inauguration, President Buchanan sent a note to nearby liquor merchants, scolding them for sending champagne in small bottles. "Pints are very inconvenient in this house," he wrote, "as the article is not used in such small quantities."

"**I** USED TO BELIEVE there were only two occasions in which the American people had regard for the privacy of the president—in prayer and in fishing. I now detect you have lost the second part."

—*HERBERT HOOVER, TO NEWSPAPER REPORTERS WATCHING HIM FISH*

On the Air

AS A RADIO BROADCASTER for the Chicago Cubs
in the 1930s, Ronald Reagan had his share of on-air
bloopers. While Reagan and a telegraph operator
were stationed in Des
Moines, Iowa, another
telegraph man watched
the baseball game live at
Chicago's Wrigley Field
and tapped out the play-by-
play in Morse code. Reagan's
partner would quickly
decipher the code and
feed it to Reagan.
Reagan's job was to use this second-hand information
to colorfully describe the game over the airwaves.
Despite this bumpy procedure, Reagan usually
stayed within a half-pitch of the game's actual pace.

During one game between the St. Louis Cardinals
and the Chicago Cubs, as famed Cardinals hurler
Dizzy Dean prepared to deliver a pitch to the Cubs'
Billy Jurges, Reagan's telegraph man handed him a
note informing him that the wire had gone dead!
Rather than tell his listeners what had happened and

risk losing them to another station, Reagan improvised. Expecting communication to be restored any moment, he described Dean's windup and announced that Jurges had fouled off the pitch. The line remained down, however, and Reagan spent the next seven minutes describing foul ball after foul ball, noting in detail the mad scrambles going on in the stands after each ball landed. Finally, his telegraph man began typing again and soon handed Reagan a note that read: "Jurges popped out on the first ball pitched."

Reagan never admitted the mix-up to his listeners, who marveled at the number of pitches the Cubs hitter had supposedly fouled off.

"WHEN POWER narrows the area of man's concern, poetry reminds him of the richness and diversity of his existence. When power corrupts, poetry cleanses."
—*JOHN F. KENNEDY, 1963*

"A PEN is certainly an excellent instrument to fix a man's attention and to inflame his ambition."
—*JOHN ADAMS, FROM A 1760 DIARY ENTRY*

"WE SPEND our time taking pills and
dedicating libraries."

—*HERBERT HOOVER, ON THE ACTIVITIES
OF FORMER PRESIDENTS*

"WE NEVER repent having eaten too little."

—*THOMAS JEFFERSON, 1825*

How's the Horse?

THREE-HUNDRED-POUND President William
Howard Taft was often the target of good-natured
humor due to his rotund figure and his eagerness to
escape the troubles of Washington. Much of
America laughed when newspapers covered Taft's
horseback-riding excursion at a mountain resort in
the Philippines. At its conclusion, the excited president wired Secretary of War Elihu Root. "Stood trip
well. Rode horseback twenty-five miles to five thousand foot elevation."

Root responded dryly, "How is the horse?"

"I DON'T KNOW a lot about politics, but I know a lot about baseball."

—RICHARD NIXON

"THE TRUTH IS, I am more of a farmer than a soldier. . . . I never went into the army without regret and never retired without pleasure."

—ULYSSES S. GRANT, 1878

"I DO DECLARE upon my honor, if this be true General Pinckney has cheated me out of my two."

—JOHN ADAMS, RESPONDING TO ACCUSATIONS THAT HE HAD SENT THOMAS PINCKNEY TO ENGLAND TO PROCURE FOUR MISTRESSES FOR THE TWO OF THEM

"THE DOCTOR has me by three strokes. But I don't care. I'm four states ahead in yesterday's election."

—WOODROW WILSON, ON THE GOLF COURSE, FOLLOWING THE 1916 ELECTION

President Adams's Daily Swim

PRESIDENT JOHN QUINCY ADAMS regularly rose well before dawn to go for a swim in the Potomac River before beginning his day in the White House. One morning the president set out with his son, John, and servant, Antoine. Adams decided to canoe across the river and then swim back, so he removed his shoes, coat, and vest for the trip, intending to fully disrobe before his return swim. Antoine stripped naked and assumed the duties of rowing the canoe. Young John doubted the vessel's seaworthiness and decided to wait ashore, then swim out to meet his father halfway on his return.

This decision proved wise, for the canoe sprung a leak and filled with water, forcing Antoine and the senior Adams into the river. As the perforated craft floated away carrying a pile of clothes, the president found himself weighed down by his soaked garments as he fought to reach the riverbank. He later recalled, rather whimsically, "while struggling for life and gasping for breath, I had ample leisure to reflect on my own indiscretion."

Unencumbered by clothing, Antoine had swum ashore easily, and when Adams finally climbed out of the water he sent his servant for help. The president was forced to surrender his clothing for Antoine's mission, however. As Antoine ran off to order the presidential carriage, young John arrived on the river's far bank and joined his father, who was shivering in the nude on the shore.

Antoine eventually returned, having found some of his and the president's clothes. The servant and the president were left to divide an odd assortment of garments between them—including, oddly enough, one of Adams's shoes—before making their inglorious trip home. Fully clothed, John decided to take a different route than that of his scantily clad father and servant.

"IF I HIT YOU, *I'm* not going to apologize,
so just bang away at me as much as you like
and say nothing in the fray."
—*THEODORE ROOSEVELT ON THE TENNIS COURT*

A Family Picnic

WHILE MANY POLITICIANS RELAX by escaping to the golf course, pursuing hobbies, or indulging in a few drinks, Richard Nixon was consumed by his profession. His office was his home, and he thought about politics virtually around the clock. His wife, Pat, told the story of the Sunday afternoon on which Nixon took his family on a picnic. It was a hot and humid day, Mrs. Nixon recalled, and, "We packed a basket and got on our holiday clothes and Dick drove us down to the Senate Office Building. We marched into his big, air-conditioned office, spread a blanket on the floor in front of his desk and sat on it to eat our lunch."

"**T**HIS, to be sure, would take us two or three years and if we should not both be cured of love in that time I think the devil would be in it."

—*THOMAS JEFFERSON, 1763. URGING HIS FRIEND JOHN PAGE TO SAIL WITH HIM TO ENGLAND, JEFFERSON ALLUDED TO HIS FEELINGS OF HOPELESSNESS IN AFFAIRS OF THE HEART.*

"THE ONLY OTHER president to have visited Ashland was Calvin Coolidge, who never said a word. I was here for only one night and spoke all the time."

—JOHN F. KENNEDY, FROM A 1963 SPEECH
IN ASHLAND, WISCONSIN

"EVERYONE CONCEDES that fish will not bite in the presence of the representatives of the press."

—HERBERT HOOVER, 1929

"YOU WILL NEVER be alone with a poet
in your pocket."

—JOHN ADAMS, FROM A 1793 LETTER
TO HIS SON, JOHN QUINCY ADAMS

"THE THINGS I want to know are in books. My best friend is the man who'll get me a book I ain't read."

—ABRAHAM LINCOLN, FROM HIS YOUTH

Shark Scare

THEODORE ROOSEVELT'S LOVE of the outdoors and enjoyment of robust physical activity were his most memorable characteristics. During the Spanish-American War, following the surrender of the Spanish garrison in Cuba in July 1898, Colonel Roosevelt decided to go for a swim in the waters of the Caribbean. He thought it would be fun to explore the wreckage of the navy collier *Merrimac,* which had been sunk about 300 yards from shore, and he asked Lieutenant Jack Greenway to join him. A few strokes into their swim, the officers heard the loud voice of General Fitzhugh Lee booming out at them from the parapet of nearby Fort Morro.

"Can you make out what he's trying to say?" Roosevelt asked Greenway between splashes.

"Sharks," answered the lieutenant nervously.

Unfazed by the threat, Roosevelt explained between strokes and occasional gulps of water how he'd been studying sharks all his life and had never heard of one bothering a swimmer. "It's all poppy-cock," he shouted above the din of rolling waves.

Lieutenant Greenway was unconvinced, especially when one sharp-toothed shark after another swam up alongside the swimmers as if waiting in ambush. Roosevelt didn't seem to notice. Meanwhile, General Lee continued to shout warnings from the fort while working feverishly to get the attention of his junior officers, whom he expected to be eaten at any moment.

The swimmers finally reached the half-submerged ship, and Roosevelt eagerly set about examining the wreck. His lieutenant remained preoccupied with the thought of their return trip to shore. Too soon for Greenway, the colonel finished with his inspection and leapt back into the water, where the men were soon surrounded once more by their shark escorts. While the old general resumed his shouting, Roosevelt and Greenway somehow navigated their way back to shore unmolested. The fearless Roosevelt had thoroughly enjoyed his excursion; his colleague was just happy to be in one piece.

Step on It!

HERBERT HOOVER, who loved to speed in his 16-cylinder Cadillac, earned a reputation as a crazed driver. One day in 1933, Hoover was stopped for speeding. His son, Allan, then took over the wheel, and when he leveled off at 85 miles per hour, his father asked him, "What's holding you back?"

"BY MY PHYSICAL constitution I am but an ordinary man.... Yet some great events, some cutting expressions, some mean hypocrisies, have at times thrown this assemblage of sloth, sleep and littleness into rage like a lion."

—*JOHN ADAMS, 1779*

"NOBODY WHO HAS tried both public and private life can doubt but that you were much happier on the banks of the Potomac than you will be at New York."

—*THOMAS JEFFERSON, FROM A 1789 LETTER TO GEORGE WASHINGTON, WHO HAD PREFERRED LIFE ON HIS FARM TO THE PRESIDENCY*

"IT WAS involuntary. They sank my boat."

—*JOHN F. KENNEDY, ON BEING ASKED HOW
HE BECAME A HERO IN WORLD WAR II*

An "Ax"idental Contest

STANDING 6' 4", Abraham Lincoln could best be described as long and lean. He did not look particularly strong, but beneath his drab garb were surprisingly powerful shoulders and taut muscles. During a visit to City Point, Virginia, near the end of the Civil War, Lincoln spent several hours shaking hands with Union soldiers.

When an army surgeon expressed concern that the president's arm must ache from the exertion, Lincoln smiled and said he had "strong muscles." To prove his point, he picked up a heavy ax and chopped away heartily at a log for several minutes. Then, taking the ax handle in one hand and holding it at its base, he extended his arm straight out horizontally and held it there without so much as flinching. Impressed, several of the stronger soldiers tried to duplicate this feat but could not.

Excuse Me . . .

AT A WHITE HOUSE DINNER honoring President Francois Mitterrand of France, Ronald and Nancy Reagan and President and Mrs. Mitterrand went through the requisite receiving line and entered the state dining room. By custom, the other guests were to remain standing until Mrs. Reagan had led President Mitterrand to his seat and President Reagan had done the same for Mrs. Mitterrand. When it was time for Reagan and Mrs. Mitterrand to go to their table, she stood frozen.

"We're supposed to go over there to the other side," Reagan mumbled awkwardly to his unmoving guest. Mrs. Mitterrand whispered something in French, which Reagan didn't understand. She repeated it, and Reagan again shook his head, uncomprehending. Suddenly an interpreter approached and told the embarrassed president, "She's telling you that you're standing on her gown."

"SPENT THE FORENOON between my library and the potato field without doing much in either."
—*JAMES A. GARFIELD, FROM AN 1879 DIARY ENTRY*

"I WON'T be long."
—*TEDDY ROOSEVELT, 1898, AS HE BOARDED A SOUTHBOUND TRAIN TO PREPARE FOR DUTY IN THE SPANISH-AMERICAN WAR*

"I COULD NEVER eat anything that went on two legs."
—*ULYSSES S. GRANT, ON HIS EATING HABITS*

Save the Date

A friend of Thomas Jefferson's, who owned a fine, strong horse, challenged him to a race. Jefferson owned a fat old mare but, surprisingly, accepted the bet. The two agreed on a date for the match. Race day had almost arrived when someone finally noticed that Jefferson had set the date of the race for February 30.

The Dutchman's

"**H**E IS THE KIND OF MAN who would rather do something badly for himself than have somebody else do it well," said Samuel J. Tilden of Grover Cleveland. Cleveland, who was the only president to be elected to a second term after losing his initial reelection bid, had enjoyed a colorful past.

Cleveland began his career in public service in 1871, when he was elected sheriff of Erie County, New York. The jovial, portly, walrus-mustached sheriff thoroughly enjoyed the barroom atmosphere, and he and his friends shared endless laughs and steins of beer in Buffalo saloons. Louis Goetz, the owner of a local bar called The Dutchman's, was a good friend of the sheriff and would often stay open for "Grofer" and company well past Buffalo's 1:00 A.M. curfew.

Cleveland, who loved to play practical jokes, dropped in at The Dutchman's one night and found Goetz asleep in a chair. The sheriff quietly turned the bar's clocks ahead two hours, then went out to find a policeman, whom he let in on his joke. Cleveland returned to the bar, woke his friend, and sat down for a drink. Moments later, the policeman walked in and told Goetz he was under arrest for serving Cleveland after curfew.

Stories of Cleveland's boisterous years in New York, along with rumors that he had fathered an illegitimate child, were thrown at him when he ran for president in 1884. The candidate's only response to the attacks was to tell the truth. In fact, his personal integrity and honesty helped him win the election. The 49-year-old Cleveland even showed a trace of his old independent spirit when he married 21-year-old Frances Folsom in 1886. He was the first and only president to marry while in the White House.

"**T**HE REASON for all is that fishing is good for the soul of man."

—*HERBERT HOOVER, 1927, ON EFFORTS TO PRESERVE FISHING GROUNDS*

"**A**THLETIC PROFICIENCY is a mighty good servant, and like so many other good servants, a mighty bad master."

—*THEODORE ROOSEVELT*

Dead Man Sleeping

WILLIAM HOWARD TAFT'S tremendous girth occasionally caused him some rather humorous problems. His prodigious appetite often left him sleepy, and he was well known for taking sudden catnaps in the midst of conducting government business. He once fell asleep while Speaker of the House Joe Cannon was leaning over his chair talking to him. Other times, when Taft nodded off in the back of the presidential automobile and the swaying of the car caused him to topple over sideways, he'd go right on snoozing.

In 1910, after a dinner at the White House with his cabinet, Taft requested that some music be played on the Victrola, but he was asleep upright in his chair within a few minutes. Upon waking he requested another song, but he dozed off again before it had even started.

As the president snored, his attorney general put on a particularly rousing piece of music, saying, "it will wake anyone but a dead man." When it ended, he noted of the still-sleeping president, "He must be dead."

Got It!

IN HIS YOUNGER YEARS, George Washington enjoyed few things more than a good fox hunt. The hours-long hunt often commenced with Washington at the head of a group of riders, tearing across the Virginia countryside on his horse. One such expedition in 1770 ended curiously enough for Washington to note it in his journal. The future president chased a fox for more than two hours and finally "captured" his quarry "after treeing her twice, the last of which time she fell dead out of the tree after being there several minutes, apparently well." Apparently natural causes had done in the spent fox.

"I AM SAVAGE enough to prefer the woods, the wilds,
and the independence of Monticello, to all the
brilliant pleasure of this gay capital."

—*THOMAS JEFFERSON, 1785, ON PARIS*

I Like Singing

RENOWNED HUMORIST Will Rogers was quite fond
of President Calvin Coolidge and felt the tight-lipped
chief executive understood the art of subtle humor
better than any other politician he had encountered.
Rogers described how he had once dropped by the

White House to invite the president to a show he was doing in the area. It would be a simple affair, Rogers informed him; there would be a couple of hours of him talking and also some work by a fine singing quartet. Coolidge then deadpanned, "Yes, I like singing."

Leftovers

CALVIN COOLIDGE'S TIGHT economic policies extended to his own financial affairs; he even liked to be able to account for leftovers in the refrigerator. Soon after meeting him, the future Mrs. Coolidge invited Calvin on a picnic with two friends and herself, but asked Cal to supply the lunch. Coolidge delivered an excellent meal of chicken sandwiches, shortcake, and macaroons. After the party finished eating, Calvin counted up the remaining macaroons and asked the others how many they had each eaten. As Mrs. Coolidge remembered years later, "Half a macaroon was missing. For it no account has ever been made."

Oval Office Gossip

In ADDITION to the various birds, dogs, and other animals sent to President Coolidge as gifts were a black-haired bear, two cubs, and a "small" hippopotamus. His favorite pet was a white collie named Rob Roy.

Innocent Until Proven Guilty

DURING HIS DAYS as a lawyer in Illinois, Abraham Lincoln generally relied on cleverness and deductive powers in the courtroom, favoring a subtle approach. His near-legendary skill in cross-examination was best displayed in one of his most famous criminal cases, the 1858 murder trial of William "Duff" Armstrong. Armstrong and James Norris had been charged with killing a man during a brawl the previous August. Norris was convicted of manslaughter, but Armstrong's mother, Hannah, asked Lincoln to defend her son. The long-limbed attorney had been friends with the defendant's father and accepted the case without charge.

The prosecution's case rested on the testimony of a man named Charles Allen, who claimed to have witnessed the night attack in the glowing light of the nearly full moon overhead. Armstrong, he said, had struck the victim in the eye with a metal slingshot and Norris had hit him with a piece of wood. When Allen took the stand, Lincoln calmly asked him to state his version of events and how he had been able to see so clearly from a distance of 150 feet. He questioned Allen closely but with apparent casualness, going over the story several times so the jury had a clear picture of the scene.

LIKE WASHINGTON, John Adams lost most of his teeth to gum disease. He refused to wear the cumbersome dentures of the period, however, and therefore talked with a lisp.

CALVIN COOLIDGE once shook hands with 1,900 people in 34 minutes; he considered this greeting marathon his personal record.

STANDING ROUGHLY 5'4" and weighing a mere 100 pounds, James Madison was our smallest president. The tallest, Abraham Lincoln, was about a foot taller, at 6'4".

MARTIN VAN BUREN was scornfully referred to by his opponents as the "Red Fox of Kinderhook" and the "Little Magician."

AN AVID SWIMMER, John Quincy Adams swam the width of the Potomac River at age 58. He also often went skinny-dipping in warm weather, taking his last nude dip at age 79.

HARDLY THE happy-go-lucky type, Benjamin Harrison was known as the "human iceberg."

JOHN ADAMS was mockingly called "His Rotundity" by some political opponents.

HERBERT HOOVER was known as "The Great Engineer" for the years he spent in the mining business. As president, he liked to take his family out into the country on picnics, where he would show them how to divert a stream by piling rocks and digging canals, covering himself in mud in the process.

ANDREW JACKSON was nicknamed "Old Hickory";
his protégé, James K. Polk, was called
"Young Hickory."

The Thirty-Minute Rule

HARRY S TRUMAN'S no-nonsense manner and
economical speaking style caught the press corps off
guard when he became president. During one of his
early press conferences, the room lapsed into a brief
silence as correspondents made notes and prepared
other queries after the opening sequence of questions.
Truman waited a few moments and, not being one
to waste time, said, "Well, I guess that's all, boys,"
and left the room. The conference had lasted just six
minutes.

Dumbfounded and somewhat embarrassed,
the assembled reporters formed a small committee,
which was sent to Truman to ask that future press
conferences last at least one half hour. Truman
agreed, and the modern thirty-minute presidential
press conference was established.

Size Does Matter

DURING HIS YEARS as ambassador to France, Thomas Jefferson found himself engaged in a debate with renowned French naturalist Georges de Buffon, who had proclaimed North American plants and animals inferior in size and quality to those of Europe. Fiercely proud of his country, and well acquainted with its animal inhabitants, Jefferson was determined to refute the claim. He declared that American deer had horns two feet long, and that "the reindeer could walk under the belly of our moose." Without regard for cost, Jefferson sent an expedition into the White Mountains with orders to return with "the skin, the skeleton, and the horns of the Moose, the Caribou, and the Original or Elk." He directed the hunters to preserve the carcasses as much as possible in order to capture the true size of the animals.

The specimens were successfully gathered, but Jefferson found them less impressive in stature than he had hoped. Accordingly, he sponsored another expedition. This one yielded a moose that was sent to Jefferson's Paris hotel. Again disappointed by the "merely" seven-foot creature, the hair of which kept falling out, Jefferson nevertheless displayed it in the hotel lobby for the five-foot-tall Buffon, who examined it and stood by his statement. The exasperated Jefferson backed off in his arguments.

KNOWN AS the "Dude President" for his stylish dress, Chester Arthur had 24 wagonloads of White House furniture and used clothing auctioned off before having the entire building redecorated. He refused to move in until this was done.

HARRY S TRUMAN, now considered one of America's best presidents, was heavily in debt by age 38 as a result of his failed haberdashery business. The year his business went under, however, Truman was elected a county judge in Missouri, and his "second career" was underway.

AT BARELY over 130 words, George Washington's second inaugural address was the shortest ever. The longest, at more than 8,000 words, was read by William Henry Harrison, who died of pneumonia one month after delivering it on an icy cold day.

AFTER LEAVING the White House, Millard Fillmore served as vice president of the Erie County, New York, branch of the Society for the Prevention of Cruelty to Animals.

ON THE DAY OF Abraham Lincoln's second inauguration, Vice President-elect Andrew Johnson felt sick. Trying to steady himself, he downed two shots of whiskey before making a short speech. He then rambled incoherently for 15 minutes. The combination of his nausea and the liquor made his first day as second-in-command one he, and the nation, would not soon forget.

AS GOVERNOR of Massachusetts,
tight-lipped Calvin Coolidge was known as the
"Silent Man on Beacon Hill."

DWIGHT D. EISENHOWER initially planned to
attend the U.S. Naval Academy but found out
at the last moment that, at age 20, he was too old
to gain admission. He was forced to "settle"
for West Point and a career in the army.

MARTIN VAN BUREN enjoyed gambling and often
bet on the outcome of elections.

PRACTICALLY BLIND without his glasses,
Harry S Truman memorized the eye chart in order
to pass his army-entrance physical and
participate in World War I.

How Ronald Became Ronald

RONALD REAGAN disliked his given name and consequently had always gone by his nickname, "Dutch." When Reagan arrived in Hollywood in 1937 to begin his film career, Warner Bros. decided its new pupil needed a new name. As press agents sat around a table proposing and rejecting one name after another, Reagan startled them with a suggestion. "How about Ronald? Ronald Reagan?"

"Hey, that's not bad," one agent said.

And so Ronald Reagan remained Ronald Reagan.

AN ARDENT CONSERVATIONIST and sponsor of the national park system, Theodore Roosevelt nevertheless loved hunting and once bagged 296 animals on an African safari.

ANDREW JOHNSON never had a day of formal schooling in his life.

LARGE-BODIED William Howard Taft once became stuck in the White House bathtub. Sometime later a new, oversized model was installed for his personal use.

AFTER LEAVING the Army in 1853, Ulysses S. Grant failed at farming, and he was working as a clerk in his father's Illinois leather goods store when the Civil War began. Seven years later, he was elected president.

THOMAS JEFFERSON trained a mockingbird to follow him around and take food from his lips.

JAMES POLK was the first president to be photographed.

JOHN QUINCY ADAMS installed the first billiard table in the White House, an act much appreciated by many of his successors.

DURING HIS TIME in the White House, Chester Arthur placed a fresh bouquet of flowers next to his deceased wife's picture every day.

DWIGHT D. EISENHOWER was considered one of the finest football players in the East during his gridiron days with West Point. Following a serious knee injury in 1912, however, he took up a sport with less tackling—golf.

HERBERT HOOVER kept a collection of 20,000 cartoons and caricatures of himself in a White House room he called his "chamber of horrors."

ANDREW JOHNSON began his career as a tailor in Tennessee, where he earned a reputation as being efficient and even stylish in his work.

A Military Man

ONE OF THE FINEST GENERALS ever produced by the United States, Ulysses S. Grant nonetheless claimed more than once that he never really considered himself a military man. He was not thrilled by his 1839 appointment to West Point. He had hoped to attain a simple job teaching mathematics before he was lulled in by the routine of army life.

In a post-presidency world tour, Grant had the opportunity to meet England's second Duke of Wellington—whose father had defeated none other than Napoleon at the Battle of Waterloo in 1815. Upon meeting the duke, Grant said, in all seriousness, "They tell me, my Lord, that your father was also a military man."

WARREN G. HARDING once saved the life of a dog who had been sentenced to death by a Pennsylvania justice of the peace. Harding surprised the governor of that state by personally appealing for clemency for the dog. The governor, of course, granted his request.

IN ORDER TO ELIMINATE concerns over protocol
and rank at White House dinners,
Thomas Jefferson had a circular table installed.

LONG BEFORE the age of sterilized medical
instruments, a teenaged James K. Polk underwent
gallstone surgery with no more than a shot of
brandy for anesthetic. He somehow survived,
and his health improved immediately.

AT THE AGE OF 15, Ronald Reagan began a seven-
year stint as a lifeguard in Dixon, Illinois, where he
was credited with rescuing 77 people.

WILLIAM HOWARD TAFT established the
presidential tradition of throwing out the first ball
to open the major-league baseball season, in 1910.

IN HIGH SCHOOL, Bill Clinton played saxophone
in a band called Three Blind Mice.

WARREN G. HARDING'S DOG, "Laddie Boy,"
sat in a chair at cabinet meetings.

HERBERT HOOVER and his aides and cabinet members played "medicine ball" every morning on the White House lawn. Hoover and his "medicine ball cabinet" played their last game on the morning of Franklin Roosevelt's inauguration in 1933, and then signed the ball, which now resides at the Herbert Hoover Library in Iowa.

AMONG A NUMBER of odd pets that roamed the White House grounds during Woodrow Wilson's years as president was a tobacco-chewing goat named "Old Ike."

ABRAHAM LINCOLN estimated that he had a rough total of one year of formal schooling. Unlike most frontier boys, he disliked hunting. He trained himself to be a lawyer, and he often surprised people by quoting from memory long passages from Shakespeare's works.

Who's the Boss?

AS A TEENAGE STUDENT at Southwest Texas State Teachers College, Lyndon Johnson took a job picking up trash. Seeking more challenging and worthwhile labor, Johnson went straight to the school president and asked him for a job. Appointed assistant to the science building janitor, Johnson was soon back in President Cecil Evans's office looking for a position there. Impressed, Evans appointed Johnson assistant to his secretary. It quickly became known around school that in order to see the president one had to gain the young assistant secretary's approval. Johnson's confident attitude gave the impression that he was far more important than he was, and he soon took a more active role under President Evans. The president wasn't quite sure what to make of the bold Texan, and told him later, "I declare you hadn't been in my office a month before I could hardly tell who was president of the school—you or me."

ANDREW JOHNSON was taught to read and write at age 18 by his 17-year-old wife, Eliza.

WHEN RONALD REAGAN arrived in Hollywood to begin his acting career, he was told that his head looked too small and his neck too short.

DURING JAMES POLK'S term in the White House, card playing, dancing, and the use of alcohol were banned.

JAMES BUCHANAN was the only president to remain a bachelor all his life. His niece, Harriet, acted as first lady throughout his term.

CHESTER ARTHUR'S last official act as president was to sign a bill that gave former president Ulysses S. Grant a full general's pension. At the time, Grant was struggling financially and dying of cancer, and the pension helped provide for the Civil War hero's wife after he died.

A THROWBACK to the previous century, Harry S Truman disdained such modern ideas as air-conditioning and Daylight Savings Time. He liked to wear two watches—one set to Eastern Standard Time and one to Missouri time.

IN 1886, 49-year-old Grover Cleveland became the first and only president to wed in the White House, when he married 21-year-old Frances Folsom.

CALVIN COOLIDGE received a mechanical horse as a gift and installed it in his bedroom at the White House, where he rode it every afternoon.

GERALD FORD was the backup center on the University of Michigan's national championship football teams in 1932 and 1933.

THOMAS **J**EFFERSON'S wine tab from his years in the White House amounted to $10,000.

THEODORE **R**OOSEVELT was the first president to receive the Nobel Peace Prize (1905) and to ride in an airplane (though not at the same time!).

JIMMY **C**ARTER was the first president to be born in a hospital.

What's in a Name?

ONE OF THE FIRST THOUGHTS of 17-year-old
Hiram Ulysses Grant as he prepared to report to the
United States Military Academy at West Point in
1839 was the opportunity he now had to change his
name. He had always preferred the grandiose sound
of Ulysses to his first name, and the fact that his
initials were H.U.G. made the idea of a change even
more appealing. Before he left home for the academy,
however, a neighbor presented him with a brand-new
steamer trunk with his initials emblazoned across it in
brass tacks. The well-intended but somewhat embarrassing gift certainly would not help Grant in his
conversion to tough, regimented military life among
other young men.

When he reached West Point, the young cadet-
to-be simply reversed his first and middle names
when he signed in and considered himself renamed.
Unbeknownst to Grant, however, the congressman
who had arranged young Ulysses's appointment to
the academy had sent Grant's paperwork to the War
Department under the name "Ulysses Simpson
Grant" because he could not remember Grant's

middle name. The congressman may have recalled that Grant's mother's maiden name was Simpson and concluded that that would serve the purpose.

In any case, Grant was informed that he was registered as Ulysses S. Grant, and that's who he would remain while in the Army. Grant gladly accepted his new identity, which eventually helped him earn another, more impressive moniker. Following Brigadier General Grant's capture of Fort Donelson in 1862, in which he had demanded in no uncertain terms the fort's capitulation, northern newspapers reported that they had discovered what the "U. S." in his name stood for: "Unconditional Surrender."

A NIGHT OWL, Chester Arthur liked to take late-night walks and rarely retired before the early-morning hours. He once set out with two associates for a 45-minute stroll through Washington, D.C., at 3:00 A.M.

GROVER CLEVELAND and Benjamin Harrison were once portrayed together in a national beer advertisement.

GEORGE WASHINGTON was the only president never to live in the White House, which did not open until 1800.

IN ORDER TO CUT down on maintenance expenses, Woodrow Wilson once kept sheep on the White House lawn to trim its grass.

HARRY S TRUMAN was known for hosting occasional marathon poker games in the White House, which often helped empty his pockets.

GEORGE BUSH was a "good-field, no-hit" first baseman on the Yale baseball team that lost the 1947 and 1948 College World Series.

JOHN F. KENNEDY was a speed-reader. He could absorb up to 2,000 words a minute, and he often read ten newspapers a day.

JOHN ADAMS and John Quincy Adams were the only father and son to hold the office of president, while William Henry Harrison and Benjamin Harrison were the only grandfather and grandson to both become chief executive.

WILLIAM HOWARD TAFT was the last president to keep a cow. "Pauline" strolled and grazed on the White House's south lawn.

FRANKLIN PIERCE recited his entire 1853 inaugural address from memory.

FOR YEARS, Jimmy Carter taught Sunday School in Plains, Georgia, and during his presidential term he sometimes taught Bible class at the First Baptist Church in Washington, D.C.

JAMES MONROE once broke up a sword duel between the British and French foreign ministers during a White House dinner.

ANDREW JACKSON was once accosted by a man who aimed his pistol at the president and pulled the trigger, but it misfired. Before Jackson could react, his assailant pulled another pistol and again fired, but, incredibly, this one also failed. The gunman was quickly subdued, and witnesses marveled at the president's luck.

JOHN QUINCY ADAMS'S diary spanned 50 years and encompassed 19 volumes of 500 pages each.

GERALD FORD once worked part-time as a model.

How to Shake Hands

THE STRAIGHTLACED James K. Polk was generally well-liked, but his lukewarm personality led people to believe he was rather dull. On one occasion, the president endeavored to explain to some White House guests how he managed the art of the hand-shake when entertaining large crowds. As his curious audience listened, Polk described in detail his differing methods of handling stronger-looking men as opposed to smaller ones, along with the "technical" aspects of shaking a hand extended either horizontally or perpendicularly. These procedures were very practical, Polk said, in that they greatly decreased the wear and tear on his own arm. The gathered crowd was heartily amused by the president's witty and humorous elaboration of the simple act of a hand-shake. Polk, however, was completely serious.

WILLIAM HENRY HARRISON'S first lady, Anna, never joined him in the White House. After delivering his one-hour-and-forty-minute inaugural address in freezing rain, Harrison became sick and died a month into his term.

PLAIN-SPEAKING Harry S Truman had only a high school education, but he was a talented pianist who enjoyed playing the works of Mozart and Beethoven.

DUE TO A PECULIAR disorder that left one of his eyes nearsighted and the other farsighted, James Buchanan's head was habitually cocked to the left.

FRANKLIN DELANO ROOSEVELT often delved into his extensive stamp collection to escape the worries of his job.

LYNDON JOHNSON enjoyed taking guests on high-speed tours of his Texas ranch in his Lincoln Continental.

BEFORE BECOMING president, Warren G. Harding made several visits to the Battle Creek Sanitarium in Ohio to recover from various nervous illnesses.

ABRAHAM LINCOLN was the only president to be awarded a patent, for an invention that allowed riverboats to more easily pass over sandbars.

THOMAS JEFFERSON sang habitually and could be heard crooning almost all the time—whenever he walked or rode his horse, and sometimes even when he read.

RICHARD NIXON'S childhood ambition was to be a railroad engineer. His hero was a Santa Fe Railroad engineer who lived in his hometown.

THE FIRST COIN bearing the likeness of a living president was the 1926 Sesquicentennial half dollar, one side of which bore the heads of Washington and Coolidge.

THOMAS JEFFERSON instituted the
practice of shaking hands instead of bowing
at White House receptions.

JAMES A. GARFIELD liked to invite friends to his
home to sing old songs.

THEODORE ROOSEVELT invited boxing champion
Mike Donovan to spar with him at the White House.
He also regularly grappled with wrestlers
and trained in the art of jujitsu.

ON JANUARY 8, 1815, General Andrew Jackson's ragged American soldiers crushed a British force at New Orleans in the most decisive American victory of the War of 1812. Unbeknownst to Jackson, the war had ended two weeks earlier.

HERBERT HOOVER'S DOG, King Tut, seemed to take after his master, who was known for his serious demeanor. After years of guarding the White House grounds, King Tut grew more sullen and stopped eating. When he died, some said that he'd worried himself to death!

RICHARD NIXON was named after King Richard the Lion-Hearted.

RONALD REAGAN and his wife, Nancy, each played their last film role in 1957's *Hellcats of the Navy*.

GROVER CLEVELAND once had secret surgery aboard a yacht in Long Island Sound for the removal of a cancerous growth from his mouth. He actually had part of his upper jaw replaced by a rubber insert and recovered nicely.

THOMAS JEFFERSON loved to experiment. Among his many inventions and innovations were the swivel chair and the "polygraph," a contraption of rods connecting two pens, which allowed him to make exact duplicates of letters as he wrote. He also invented an efficient plow moldboard, which earned him a medal from a French agricultural society.

AT THE AGE OF NINE, Andrew Jackson was selected as a "public reader" for those who could not read in his home village, and he read the Declaration of Independence aloud from a Philadelphia newspaper to his excited elders.